FRONTIERS OF
JAZZ

FRONTIERS OF
JAZZ

THIRD REVISED EDITION

Edited by
Ralph de Toledano

PELICAN PUBLISHING COMPANY
Gretna 1994

The word "Pelican" and the depiction of a pelican are
trademarks of Pelican Publishing Company, Inc., and are
registered in the U.S. Patent and Trademark Office.

Harpsichords and Jazz Trumpets, copyright July, September 1934 by Lincoln Kerstein / *The Blues,* copyright 1962 by A. and C. Boni / *They Sang in Jazz,* reprinted by permission of the National Review / *I Discovered Jazz in 1902,* copyright 1938 by Downbeat, Inc. / *Duke Ellington,* copyright 1933 by Fortune, Inc. / *Benny Goodman and the Swing Period,* copyright 1938 by Frank Norris / *Piano in the Bank,* copyright 1947 by Dorothy Chamberlain.

LIBRARY OF CONGRESS CATALOGING IN PUBLICATION DATA

Frontiers of jazz / edited by Ralph de Toledano. — 3rd ed.
    p.   cm.
    Includes index.
    ISBN 1-56554-043-3
    1. Jazz—History and criticism. 2. Jazz musicians. I. Toledano, Ralph de, 1916- .
ML3506.F76 1994
781.65—dc20   93-42542
                                   CIP
                                   MN

Manufactured in the United States of America

Published by Pelican Publishing Company, Inc.
1101 Monroe Street, Gretna, Louisiana 70053

Contents

PREFACE, by Milton Gabler   vii

EDITOR'S INTRODUCTION, by Ralph de Toledano   xii

THE DIRECTIONS OF JAZZ,   1
by Ralph de Toledano

HARPSICHORDS & JAZZ TRUMPETS,   11
by Roger Pryor Dodge, from *Hound and Horn*

THE BLUES,   30
by Abbe Niles, from *The Blues*

NOTES ON BOOGIE WOOGIE,   56
by William Russell, from *HRS Rag*

JAZZ IN AMERICA,   64
by Jean-Paul Sartre, from *Les Cahiers America*

THEY SANG IN JAZZ,   67
by Ralph de Toledano, from *National Review*

KING OLIVER,   71
by Preston Jackson, from *Hot News*

THE NEW ORLEANS RHYTHM KINGS,   78
by George Beall, from *Swing Music*

JAZZ PRE-HISTORY, AND BUNK JOHNSON,   87
by Morroe Berger

I DISCOVERED JAZZ IN 1902,   100
by Jelly Roll Morton, from *Downbeat*

JELLY ROLL MORTON ON RECORDS,   104
by Hughes Panassie, from *Jazz Information*

BECHET & JAZZ VISIT EUROPE, 1919,   111
by Ernst-Alexandre Ansermet, from *Revue Romande*

LOUIS ARMSTRONG: A REMINISCENCE,   119
by Bud Freeman

THE WOLVERINES AND BIX,   123
by George Johnson, from *Swing Music* and *Downbeat*

DUKE ELLINGTON,   137
by Wilder Hobson, from *Fortune*

BENNY GOODMAN AND THE SWING PERIOD,   148
by Frank Norris, from the *Saturday Evening Post*

PIANO IN THE BAND,   162
   by Otis Ferguson, from the *New Republic*
GRANDFATHER OF HOT PIANO,   170
   by Ross Russell
INDEX   177

Preface

JAZZ, CRITICS, AND THIS BOOK

A T the present time there are a great many record collectors and jazz fanciers who have not had the opportunity to read all of the old articles or hear all of the old bands and soloists. I doubt if there is any one person who has been that fortunate. There was a time, in the early thirties, when I myself would regret not having been old enough to hear the great men making music only five to ten years prior to my awareness of their existence. Still, I heard an awful lot of live music along with the canned, for in those days records of what had gone before were not impossible to obtain. Now fifteen years have passed and to the new collector it is a quarter century—with time and thousands of new fans making it almost impossible to catch up with the past.

Of course, the new fans have the written word. There are dozens of periodicals and books on the subject. In the golden era there was only the music, and you had to make up your own mind as to whether it was right and righteous. So it is up to us, the old timers, the first jitterbugs, to set it down on paper and spread the gospel. Being a normal person of average intelligence, I may safely assume that if I like a particular type of music, there must be thousands of uninitiated who would enjoy it too, if it were brought to their attention. Therefore this collection of rare jazz literature is as important as the music, and a stepping stone in the education of the jazz lover.

I have been associated with these flat round concentric objects, the men that make them, and the people that play them for the past twenty years. I know most of them personally and someone once tabbed me the critic's critic. My place (the Commodore Music Shop) was a haven for them. Perhaps it was the only place they could go to relax or argue. They all came to me and I listened and learned. So, I know Wilder Hobson, Frank Norris, John Hammond, Hugues Panassié, Helen Oakley, George Frazier, Leonard Feather, Stanley Dance, Eugene Williams, William

Russell, Bill Love, Fred Ramsey, Charles Edward Smith, Rudi Blesh, Otis Ferguson, Nesuhi Ertegun, Ross Russell, Norman Granz, Ernest Anderson, Charles Delaunay, Dave Dexter, George Simon, Barry Ulanov, Robert Goffin, Ralph Berton, George Avakian, etc., etc., and Louis Armstrong, Jelly Roll Morton, Duke Ellington, Benny Goodman, both Dorseys, Count Basie, Woody Herman, Lionel Hampton, Fats Waller, Sidney Bechet, Milt Mezzrow, Eddie Condon, Zutty Singleton, George Wettling, Gene Krupa, Billie Holiday, George Brunis, Muggsy Spanier, Joe Sullivan, Jess Stacy, Pee Wee Russell, Mel Powell, Eddie Edwards, and hundreds of others as well as the Scarsdale High School Jazz Band, newcomers that are making their mark. I have listened to all of them and find that jazz is not on the way out. There are more people buying it and listening to it now than ever before. They must hear something that outsiders do not hear. If you are an outsider perhaps you hear but don't listen. There is a difference, and it is up to you. Lend me your ears! But first, lend me your eyes, your mind, and some free time. Time enough to read the following notes, originally written for a show at Town Hall, on February 21st, 1942. The proceedings were billed as "A CHIAROSCURO JAZZ CONCERT. Supervised by EDDIE CONDON." Maybe you'll get my drift. Perhaps my story will help you to understand and not be an "outsider."

Don't ever let anyone hear you say that Jazz is on the way out. For after all, to be on the way out it first must have come in. And brethren as far as I know, this music, yes—I said *music,* never had a chance to prove itself. Don't tell me about big bands 'cause they just don't play jazz; and small bands, the public just won't listen to 'em. You know what I mean, they sound too noisy,—that is to the public. It seems people will not take the time to open their ears. That's the trouble. So what? So Jazz suffers.

Let me tell you about a friend of mine, he says, "Gabe, let's take in this concert, this Chiaroscuro Jazz Concert." So I ask him and he tells me that chiaroscuro is the arrangement of light and dark parts, like in a picture. So this concert must be the arrangement of Negro and white musicians on the stage, only there won't be any arrangements, if you get what I mean. Getting back to this friend of mine, he also says, "You're the guy who's supposed to understand all this, maybe you can enlighten me. Maybe for once, I'll be able to enjoy what I hear." "O.K." I says, "but don't hope for too much. After all, half of the time I don't get what's happening myself." How can I expect him to recognize a good version of *Muscrat Ramble,* if I myself, "The Gabe," am not sure whether it's *Muscrat Ramble* or *Da Da Strain,* excepting by this time I've heard *Muscrat* at least a thousand different times and after a couple of bad guesses get it right by asking some guy in the band. Sure, I'm supposed to be the smart one, even if I tell him it's the *Chattanooga Choo Choo Stomp,* he believes me. The Great Mahoska, that's me. I can't be wrong. Then again, I generally know the name of the tune because I request it, or I hear them pass the title around before they start, something like, *Baby in F,* for *I've Found A New Baby* in the key of F. There's nothing to it, if your ears are long enough.

So you wonder why more people don't like Dixieland Jazz? That's an easy one. Most of them don't know what's going on. How can they tell what's happening to a tune that they are unfamiliar with in the first place? Maybe they think that it's supposed to be that way, when the boys get off on a particularly good one. To really feel funny inside and thrill all over you've got to follow the tune, and you can't do it when you don't know the tune. That's why Harlem Jazz is so much more commercial, there's less going on, and therefore it's easier to understand. The soloist is getting off,[1] sure he is, but what's going on behind him, nothing maybe but some fine rhythm plus an easy going riff (figure). Brother, there's nothing in it to jar your nerves. That's one sure way of telling that it's not Dixieland.

Did you ever try to relax while some fine horns were blowing, like for instance, Maxy, Pee Wee, and Brad? Man, it's impossible. Here are three men taking off, but good. To listen to any one of them individually is enough to make you melt inside, but three at a time and each of them going his own righteous way, Hell, that's better than any straight music you've ever heard. Imagine, three composers, all with the same feeling, all in the same groove, writing and playing at the same instant, playing new thoughts simultaneously, and interweaving them without ever getting in each other's way. Brother, that's music, that's the best music. Now you know why I get so excited when I hear it, but it's got to be right. There's nothing worse than bad Dixieland. Take it from me.

[1] Improvising on the melody.

Are you getting interested? Do you still follow me? Here, perhaps
I can make it a little easier for you. Understand this, trying to define
Jazz or Swing is like trying to define poetry. What is poetry? You tell
me. I recognize it when I see it, the same as I dig [2] good Jazz when I hear
it. Some people write poetry and some people just write. It's that certain
spark inside that makes the difference. You either can swing or you can't.
There is no half way. A good jazz man actually composes as he plays.
Did you ever try to play a melody and not play it at the same time? Did
you ever try to do this and keep a steady beat with good drive, or lift,
to it, not necessarily fast? It can be at any tempo, any comfortable tempo.
If you have and succeeded, you're my man.

Now take a tune, an easy one, that is one everyone knows. Take
Honeysuckle Rose for instance, that's been kicked around enough, and
"Fats" Waller wouldn't mind, even if he were here to hear it. Every
man, woman, and child in the business has worked out on it so often,
it's tired. Now listen to it. That Coleman Hawkins really tears it apart,
doesn't he? It's more beautiful than the original and still you can follow
it. It's *Honeysuckle Rose* Hawkins style. You liked it didn't you? Why?
I'll tell you why, because you could follow the tune. You knew it,
hummed it to yourself, compared it to the melody Coleman was playing,
and Coleman won. That's nothing new, he'll win every time. That is
how to listen, compare the improvisation with the original. If you liked
that, then I've hopes for you. Someday you might like Dixieland, when
you open your ears and learn the tunes. And they *are* great tunes, tunes
that were written for men to play their hearts out on.

Take my word for it, the day is coming, Dixieland will be back, and
it's something to look forward to. That'll be the day guys like Eddie,
and Pee Wee, and Max, and George, and Zutty will make money and
hold their heads high. Not that they haven't got those heads up there
now. Way up. And then, maybe Louie [3] will come back and play again.
Like he used to when these men were first inspired. There you have
something to look forward to.

But now, let us get back to the subject at hand, this book, and its
mentor.

[2] Know.
[3] Louis Armstrong, the King of them all.

As a dealer in dated discs I came in contact with dozens of music lovers who were serious enough to put their findings in print. Some came to me raw, some half baked, and some too far gone to pay attention to. The colleges of our country are blessed with campus publications and it was my good fortune to meet many young writers thirsty for the righteous nectar. Generally they lit on only one phase of the subject, specialized, and became literary spearheads for their particular pleasures, blossoming as followers of Ellington, Goodman, The Condon Gang, or Jelly-Roll Morton, Louis, Oliver, and Bunk. However, a few held to the course and appreciated all of the music. There was just one requisite, it had to be good. Toledano was one such man. I first met him when he was a student at Columbia. There was a Jazz clique up there at the time, and Ralph was only one of a group of intelligent fans. Still he never got in my hair (I had hair at that time), and if any one man is qualified to edit and classify a collection of articles for the enlightenment of the new jazz devotee, he is the one. I shall take great pleasure in meeting again my old friends between these covers, along with the ones I missed and the new words of wisdom on the subject that is closest to my heart.

MILTON GABLER

Introduction

SOME people collect butterflies. Others collect records. Butterfly collectors bother no one but the butterflies, but record collectors have driven a whole generation of small merchants, junk dealers, and respectable householders—not to mention the musicians who make the assorted sounds on the records—quite gray and a little mad. For the record collector is persistent, inspired by a fanatic zeal and the feeling that time's chariot is at his heels, bearing all the other record collectors.

Whatever the faults of collectors, and they have many, there has been method to their madness. The painstaking efforts to dig up every bit of recorded hot jazz, to classify, sort, and analyze it, and the ceaseless research to determine what musicians played on what dates, has helped unfold the history and development of jazz, steadily pushing back the limits of its pre-history. Reading the literature of jazz, from 1919 to the present, one is struck by the realization that there was little real knowledge until the record collectors began their investigations. So that every anthology of jazz criticism must make its curtsey to that rare breed of men who thrive on the dust of Salvation Army depots, hock shops, thrift shops, and the backwaters of the record trade, who live for the pleasure of turning up an unknown master, a well-known soloist on a forgotten label, who feel that of such is the kingdom of heaven if they unearth a cache of Claxtonolas or a King Oliver Gennett.

The madness of jazz collectors, however, does not stop at records. As the disease progresses, it takes in other ramifications of jazz. The urge to encompass the whole field sets in, and the collectors find other, fascinating goals. Old record catalogues have begun to assume value, or dust jackets, any of the incunabula of the consuming passion, jazz. I still remember the look of pleasure on the face of Art Hodes, who combines playing with collecting, when I gave him half a dozen ancient Melrose stock arrangements of jazz standards "as played by King Oliver" or "from the Jelly-Roll Morton phonograph recording."

Some of the urges to collect around jazz have a definitely more significant basis. In this category is the search after printed material on hot music: historical, critical, or insulting. It was this sort of collecting which led to this book. For *Frontiers of Jazz* did not spring full-pano-plied from the head of its editor. It was something that kicked around in his mind more and more persistently as his file drawer began to over-flow with clippings out of *Downbeat* and *Tempo,* articles torn out of the *Saturday Evening Post* or *The New Republic,* some beat-up pages out of *Fortune* and assorted issues of the *HRS Rag.* It was a threatening ac-cumulation as more old material turned up and more new material was published.

When, with Eugene Williams and Ralph Gleason, I was associated in the parturition, birth, and publication of *Jazz Information,* the thought occurred to me that it might be a good idea to issue reprints of the his-torical and critical writings of jazz, all in uniform size, which could be bound into one or more volumes. The plan in mind, discussed with Milt Gabler, might have come to fruition but for the dissolution of the Williams-Gleason-Toledano axis—somewhat one-sidedly reported in *Jazz Information*—and the little matter of a war. *Frontiers of Jazz* was the logical extension of the original scheme.

What I have tried to do in this volume is to bring together a collection of articles on jazz, critical and biographical articles which have been of some importance, which in their day have caused widespread comment, which in this year of our Lord still have pertinence although the mark of time may be upon them. The validity of the *Fortune* piece on Elling-ton, for instance, is remarkable, even though it appeared in the early thirties. The Roger Pryor Dodge essay, linking the pre-Bach musical tradition to certain aspects of jazz improvisation and polyphony, hardly dates at all—despite the flow of super-erudition which has developed this theme *ad absurdum.* The discussions of the Wolverines by George Johnson and of Joe Oliver by Preston Jackson, first published in Eng-land, exist as direct reportage of an era by men who lived through it as musicians. The Ansermet critique broadcasts an article written in 1919 but long known only by reputation. The critique on boogie-woogie was the only really pertinent writing I could find on that subject. And so on down the table of contents.

It seemed obvious that something would have to be done about the Bunk Johnson cult which has begun to dominate in the critical field. Morroe Berger, in summing up and evaluating the Bunk legend, expresses in part the sentiments of many old and great New Orleans musicians. Berger talked to many of the forgotten virtuosi of the Golden Age of New Orleans jazz, and in writing of Bunk, he is also telling their story.

The original job of choosing what merited inclusion and what did not was never an easy one. There was, first of all, the problem of getting permission to reprint from publishers and writers. In some cases, this was impossible. When the 1947 edition of *Frontiers of Jazz* appeared, I was criticized for not including material which I had wanted but could not get. In preparing this revised edition, I have eliminated one article which had lost its validity. I have also brought up to date my own contribution, *The Directions of Jazz,* added a needed appreciation of Bessie Smith and Billie Holiday, and included Jean-Paul Sartre's sardonic appraisal of *Jazz in America.*

It might be said that Milt Gabler's foreword has been outdistanced by the new developments in jazz. But I know of no better evocation of his zest for the music he did so much to promote. His interest in this book made it possible, and he deserves a place in it. I owe thanks to Oliver Durrell, who supervised the publication of the 1947 edition with keen understanding of the jazz field. Thanks must also go to the editors, publishers, and writers who granted me permission to re-publish material they controlled.

RALPH DE TOLEDANO.

The Directions of Jazz

RALPH de TOLEDANO

I

For a young art, jazz is full of hoary truisms. One of the hoariest is that jazz is performance. This, of course, is like saying that painting is performance. But how then differentiate between pointillism and cubism? Or in music between the improvisations of Frescobaldi and those of Jelly Roll Morton? Memory, more than meticulous scoring, keeps a musical tradition alive.

But when you've said this, the hoary truism remains. Jazz *is* performance; and the history of jazz becomes the compilation of those specific performances—and types of performance—which were preserved. I remember sitting in a recording studio some twenty-five years ago, listening to a group of men from Duke Ellington's band playing lovely, lyric rings around the tune *I Can't Give You Anything But Love*. When they had finished, the recording engineer (who thought the men were rehearsing) walked out of the booth. "I guess we should have cut that one," he said. The performance was lost forever.

It was as lost as the singing of the deep, plangorous *saeta* of Holy Week in Sevilla or the thousand ringing verses of some buried *chanson de geste*. It was as lost as all jazz would have been but for the development of the phonograph. Only because this development ran concurrently with the second, or classic, period of jazz do we know how the titans of the 1920's and 1930's sounded—or at least what they sounded like through the filter of old acoustical and early electrical recording. The phonograph allows us to trace the course of jazz since that remote era, to note the new trends and decadent influence in this exciting and allusive music.

But this analysis, whatever it may teach us of what jazz *was*, fails to offer an answer to the perennial question plaguing critics: Does

1

jazz have a future? It was asked many years ago when the Original Dixieland Jazz Band created its small explosion at the now-defunct Riesenweber's Restaurant in New York City, forcing the musical world to give it serious attention. It is asked again today after every "progressive" group debuts, finds its followers, and fades away. In the early days of discovery, when the word "jazz" expressed everything from a King Oliver solo to the flighty morals of John Held flappers, the answers were very simple. Jazz was Art—slightly eccentric, like *batik* painting perhaps—and as Art would by its very nature be self-perpetuating.

The "jazz as art" movement has thrived ever since Paul Whiteman, brandishing an outsize baton, stood before his orchestra in Aeolian Hall in 1924 to present the world with George Gershwin's *Rhapsody in Blue*. He was not the first to invade the sanctuaries of "serious" music—Will Marion Cook had taken a Negro jazz orchestra in 1919 to tour Europe's concert halls—but he got credit for the innovation. In time, Louis Armstrong aimed his long brass horn at the chandeliers of the Salle Pleyel, Duke Ellington was heard in Euterpe's staidest environs, Benny Goodman rocked Carnegie Hall, and the "jazz concert" became a commonplace. From the first, the "jazz as art" movement was afflicted by the plaudits of great musicians who also happened to be jazz illiterates—and by the senseless attacks of academicians whose idea of the real product was Henry Busse's sour rendition of *Hot Lips*. When a studious commentator discovered that there was a schematic relationship between the so-called Chicago style and the polyphony of Bach, the faddists were off in a blizzard of misapprehension.

To be fair about it, neither the public nor the critics were very much to blame. Americans have always been self-conscious about what they consider the smallness of their artistic contribution to the world. The pre-World War I literary boom had subsided, the best American writers were "following the dollar" as expatriates in France and Spain, and American letters had fallen into the hands of very poor receivers. A great deal of American art was neither American nor art. And music in the larger forms had arrived at a superlative of pretension and dullness in its third-rate imitations of second-rate carbons of the current Continental mode.

The faddists were desperately in need of something which could give them new esthetic vapors, and the general public panted along with them. They were ready for that miscegenetic marriage of jazz to Whiteman which resulted in the still-birth of "symphonic jazz"—whether by Gershwin, Ferde Grofé, or their many successors. The literature of the period is full of enthusiastic comment on the theory of symphonic jazz, most of which boiled down to several earth-shaking facts: that Shostakovitch had interpolated jazz themes in his work (Khatchaturian much more openly uses complete American popular tunes in his scores today); that Stravinsky employed certain elements of ragtime in his compositions; that Brahms was attracted to the rhythmic effects of 1890 jazz and even contemplated using them; and that the fast movement of Beethoven's Piano Sonata *Opus 111* antedated the furious pianistic gyrations of the ragtime school. With this encouragement added to the tinkle of the cash register, hacks who thought that jazz was nothing more than the "blue" effect of flatted thirds and sevenths began to turn out jazz tone poems by the vard—while critics who would have turned up their noses at such simple lack of competence in academic forms raved over a "renascence."

(Even the sound composers—men like Darius Mildhaud, for example, who thought he was writing jazz in *La Création du monde*—were taken in and added their mite to the confusion.)

Carl Sandburg, in his quiet way, put them all in their place by writing in one of his poems that "jazz is the laugh of a golden frog with a sliver of moon lost in its belly."

II

While saxophones and penny whistles screamed against an acre of violins in every concert hall from here to Stokowski, the real jazz took refuge in the honky-tonks along the Mississippi, the joints of Memphis and Harlem, the dives of Kansas City and Cicero, and the jam sessions of hot musicians who felt that playing stock arrangements from 9 at night to 3 in the morning was no particular way to live. Underground among the whites, and out of sight (though a pertinent part of their lives) among Negroes, there existed a school of music governed by an inclusive set of criteria—none of which took in the cash register or the cheers of an undisciplined generation excited by the effects of rhythm on the urino-genital system. The jazz that was played in the *hot* school reached a small group of lay listeners who sought it out and cherished it. But in the main it was a musicians' music as far as the white world was concerned, which means that it did not flourish then nor could it offer a reasonable living to those who were of its persuasion. Even today, the uncompromising hot musician finds it hard to make a living playing the music he believes in. Unless he is also a showman like Louis Armstrong, a businessman like Eddie Condon, or an institution like Ellington, he must struggle or be absorbed into the outright commercial or quasi-jazz field.

Significantly, the jazz-as-art-critics of the late swing era were sadly unaware that the boundaries of jazz went beyond Benny Goodman or Count Basie. They were not alone. The majority of those who expressed themselves in print could not see beyond Harry James and looked down upon the real jazzmen as musical illiterates. The turning point began with the publication of *Jazz Information,* the researches of William Russell and the late Eugene Williams, and the release by Milt Gabler of a series of memorable, collectively-improvised records— all in the late 1930's and early 1940's. Even in the postwar years, *Metronome,* a musicians' magazine presumably, declared war on Bunk Johnson, the old-time Negro trumpet genius, as antediluvian— and dismissed the lovers of New Orleans jazz as "moldy figs." But it went into rhapsodies over each new version of the 4-brass-4-reed-4-rhythm (plus strings) aggregation.

From a historical viewpoint, *Metronome's* "modern" exclusivists were back in the early Thirties when a combination of events set off the "swing" craze. It is curious to note that the misunderstanding of "swing" was as profound and absurd as the unseemly enthusiasms for the "jazz qualities" of Whiteman and Vincent Lopez in the "symphonic" days. When swing blew in on the tail of the Riley-Farley *Music Goes Round and Round,* the critics began digging for adjectives once they had gotten over the initial shock of discovering that it was not an extension of pseudo-experimentation in the symphonic-sonata style of Gershwin's works for large orchestra. They accepted swing as the last step in the artistic evolution of jazz.

Actually, swing was merely a simplification for popular consumption of jazz harmonies, jazz counterpoint, and most important, of jazz performance and improvisation. In a medium essentially fitted to small instrumentation ("More than eight men," a musician once told me, "and it ain't jazz"), swing substituted the large band. Of necessity this diluted the jazz element by setting the written arrangement and the instrumental blend and precision of each section—reed, brass, rhythm—above free improvisation in the idiom of individual musicians. The Lunceford band which came to the fore in the late Thirties played with tremendous drive—and its brass section, trained to an incredibly coordinated vibrato, achieved a masterly precision. It was a "swing" band but it moved steadily away from the jazz which its sidemen could have played. For the general public, the virtue of swing was that it tightened up the 6/8-over-2/4 jazz beat to a steady 4/4, and by sheer volume delineated (though by suggestion) the subtle patterns of hot jazz.

III

By the mid-1940's, swing had come to mean anything in which the big bass drum was predominant, especially if it was loud and fast. The "blues" element was driven out by Tin Pan Alley. Even the grandiose spectacle of a hundred frothing men being whipped up and down innumerable arpeggios by Andre Kostelanetz was called "swing." These excesses aside, the phenomena did result in the creation of notable moments when jazz soloists, cutting loose, recalled the initial sources of jazz. We had them when, out of a beautifully manicured Ellington arrangement, Cootie Williams' "jungle style" trumpet burst forth or Barney Bigard's rich and melodic clarinet traced musical arabesques in the air. We had them at the Benny Goodman Carnegie Hall concert in 1938, during the raucously stimulating *Sing, Sing, Sing,* when Jess Stacey's piano solo quieted the house, jazz right down to the ground, involved and delicate and full, as original as Chopin playing barrelhouse.

In the excitement of these occasions it was possible to forget that the scored arrangements surrounding the improvised solos were usually trivial, uninteresting, and sometimes in bad taste. But to carry over this momentary forgetfulness into a critical system, as many jazz enthusiasts did, betrayed the absence of any esthetic sense and the presence of an ear attuned solely to the commercial ring. To be completely fair about it, the "swing" critics did encourage the clarinet-and-string-quartet experiments of Artie Shaw and the *jeux d'esprit* of the small John Kirby band. Nevertheless "swing" moved from one form of vulgarization and exhibitionism to another—landing in the *ennui* of "bebop" music, usually based on a repeated phrase or series of phrases with "modernist" pretensions. To watch earnest collegians discussing "bebop" with all the seriousness Fritz Stiedry brought to a Bach fugue was a gruesome experience.

Within the field of legitimate hot jazz, however, certain trends were observable in the late Forties. It has already been noted that under the recurring waves of misguided passion for the by-products of jazz, whether "symphonic" or "swing," a steady current of the real music persisted. During the Twenties, in the back-alleys of the Prohibition era, and in the Thirties, when the Depression knocked a hole in the night club business, jazz went its way unconscious and uncaring. It developed according to the inclinations and the genius of the men who made it. In those days you had to know your way around to find jazz, in after-hours joints and at unpremeditated jam sessions, but what you heard was usually worth the search. This was changed by the advent of a school of dogmatic and single-track critics, plus the inevitable rivalries and comparisons which arose from the investigation and analysis of jazz history. From that point on, jazz tended to become self-conscious.

The germinal factors involved were many and complex. The impact among critics of *Jazz Information,* already mentioned; the publication in 1939 of *Jazzmen* which pioneered in the exposition of historical roots; the gradual alienation of jazz from its sources; the influx of young musicians, many Juilliard trained, whose prodigious technique was in inverse ratio to their feeling for the old jazz; popular pressure for innovation, whether good or bad—all these played their part. In the resultant chaos, critics and musicians began to divide into three distinct and antagonistic categories: the first eclectic and evolutionary; the second, a highly intellectual back-to-the-womb coterie which surrounded Bunk Johnson and made a cult of the New Orleans sexagenarians; the third, those nervous and compulsive synthesizers of urbanized jazz, modernism, and "progressivism."

IV

The spokesmen of the New Orleans group, calling themselves purists, rejected almost everything that had happened since the middle Twenties, and their followers among musicians attempted to duplicate the early playing of the masters. They scorned so-called white jazz and developed some specious race theories which held that jazz can only be played by Negroes; that in the hands of whites it ceases to be jazz; that only Negroes have an accurate sense of the true jazz beat; that the best a white jazzman can do is to make himself, à la Mezz Mezzrow, as much a Negro as he possibly can.

Some of the prophets of this school even renounced further critical writing in favor of an obscurantist *mystique,* seeing jazz as a kind of religious experience. Others, more articulate and less modest, such as the critic-entrepreneur Rudi Blesh, wrote of Negro jazz as "the application of pentatonic thinking to our diatonic scale," observed its "polymetric rhythm," and noted its "allusive" relation to "the medieval polyphony of Europe, the cantus firmus." To most musicians this was jabberwock, but it had its effect on many who made an effort to return to simple blues in the New Orleans tradition, to the marches, jazz spirituals, and burying tunes of a past era. The music they produced was sometimes very lovely to hear, but it was static, a retrogression, feeding on itself, uncreative, and by its lack of dynamism bound to disappear.

The eclectics—those non-commercial jazzmen who were not interested in theories or in musicological research, but who sought to play hot music as they felt it and to the best of the abilities—may have held the future of jazz in their hands. For it is in the direction they took that jazz must go, if it goes anywhere at all. When jazz was rediscovered in the middle Thirties, these jazzmen were acclaimed far and wide. They went into partial eclipse when the faddists on a New Orleans kick moved over to Bunk Johnson. The music they played, however, had been filtered through life and environment. As it traveled north, the French-Spanish-African accent had been modified

by the English folk song of the coastal regions, by the harsher growl
of the urbanized Negro of Memphis and Chicago, by the urban Jew
in New York, by Tin Pan Alley. Its harmonies and instrumental
techniques were conditioned by hundreds of musicians, playing in all
the jazz and quasi-jazz styles, who had sat in at thousands of jam
sessions and recording dates. It had felt the demands of the dance
band. If these influences worked on the jazz idiom, jazz was not
the loser but had gained in the semi-conscious way of all growing arts.
The eclectic jazzmen understood this.

But the eclectics were, for the most part, middle-aged men. They
could not command the wave of young musicians to subside. The
young musicians were trained or dominated by the academy. Dis-
daining the word "hot," they called themselves "cool" or "progressive"
jazzmen. They began to break down the scale, to fragment the beat,
to discard the great melodic legacy of jazz. Their improvisations,
adrenalinized and twitchy, became so intricate and so removed from the
solid harmonic traditions of the older jazz, that they made impossible
any spontaneous collective counterpoint. Gradually, the solo, played
against the muted chording of the other instruments, took over. Words
like "atonality" crept into the jazz jargon—and the aim of the ambitious "cool" jazzmen was to amaze rather than to reach those who
heard him. A few—the sincere and talented Gerry Mulligan was one
of them—never forgot that jazz must be wedded to the dance if it
is to be valid. But most of them, like André Previn, could not hear
the music for the notes.

Oddly enough, the "cool" trend did not begin with the bright
young men who eventually made up the "progressive" school. Its
genesis was in part a historical accident. In the late Thirties, Milton
Gabler, to whom jazz still owes a great debt, opened a branch of his
famous Commodore Music Shop on New York's 52nd Street—"Swing
Street" before the strippers and the office buildings took it over. Jazz
musicians from bands playing at the Famous Door, the Onyx Club,
and the other *boîtes à musique* congregated at Gabler's emporium to
gossip and to hear the latest records. While the critics, who also made
the Commodore Music Shop a kind of club, traded discographic
information or touted their latest discovery, the musicians crowded into
the booths. And because their curiosity extended beyond the limits
of jazz, they began to listen to what we call "serious" music.

Stravinsky seemed to fascinate them most—and it was a sight to see four or five jazzmen crowded into one small booth, nodding their heads approvingly and exclaiming excitedly over *Le Sacre de printemps* or *Petrouchka*. Dizzy Gillespie, not yet the leader of a bearded cult, was particularly susceptible to this "new" music—and within a short time his wild improvisations reflected what he had heard. But there were others who went the same way—and Benny Goodman's interest in Bartok sped them on. The bright young men, already oriented to the moderns, merely took over what others had begun and pushed it to its illogical extreme.

But another factor was operative in the rise and success of "progressive" jazz. The New Orleans, Chicago, and Dixieland modes had run their course. The music was not dead and it still had its loyal followers. But it had gone as far as it could go. Its practitioners were repeating themselves. The fertile creative spirit of those who made jazz was seeking for new ways of expression. They had tried to give jazz a new texture by introducing instrumentation not then part of the small band—the oboe, the French horn, the harpischord. But this was not enough—and jazz moved to Birdland.

V

The failure of "progressive" jazz was not in its innovation but in its imitation. It attempted to do badly in a night club or at a record session what the "serious" composer did much better on paper. (Duke Ellington's far more tutored efforts to blend a big-band idiom with Debussy had been no more successful). The "cooler" the music got, the more frenetically mannered and artificial it became. It had already started on the decline when the entertainment business turned away from bands and instrumentalists in favor of rock-and-rolling singers and stand-up comedians. Television, which captured the public's span of attention, struck the most serious blow. Preoccupied with gunslingers and private eyes, it found no time for jazz, hot or cool.

There are still places left where you can hear jazz—and the phonograph continues to keep the old and new music alive. Benny Goodman and Louis Armstrong can still fill a theatre or receive the dubious accolade of a guest appearance on a television variety show. Does this

mean that jazz is moribund? I do not believe so. The pessimists have
been predicting its death since the 1920's—but it has managed to sur-
vive and to grow richer. Perhaps it should be said that jazz is going
through one of its periods of hibernation, that it will emerge lean
and eager to face a new Spring. For jazz is more than a way of fingering an instrument, of striking a note, of weaving a musical pattern.
It is a totally American expression whose complex beat and lyric voice
reflect the American spirit. In a sense, it is a musical melting pot—
and when the sludge of commercialism and artiness is skimmed off,
the bright metal remains. For much of the world, jazz is America—
and in Moscow, as I have seen, a jazz record is a treasured possession.

What direction tomorrow's jazz will take is anybody's guess. But
one prediction can safely be made: The African rhythms which merged
with the English four-part hymn, the folk melodies of France and
Spain, the blues and spirituals, the flooding melody of Tin Pan Alley,
and the musical multiplicity of this country, will not strain at other
elements it picks up along the way. What "progressive" jazz added—
not the extremes but the real and true—will take its place in the legitimate tradition. Even rock 'n' roll, with its looser beat and hypnotic
surge, will leave its mark on the future jazz. In fact, jazz will thrive
on these new elements, once they are assimilated, just so long as it is
not smothered by the contrived and the self-conscious. As long as this
is avoided, jazz will not plunge into the great and dangerous pitfall,
underscored by Ezra Pound's often-quoted warning that "music begins
to atrophy when it departs too far from the dance."

"The world's jazz crazy," Mamie Smith used to sing. "Lawdy, so
am I." There is madness enough in the world, but jazz is one magnificent obsession that America will not lightly surrender.

Harpsichords and Jazz Trumpets

ROGER PRYOR DODGE
from *Hound & Horn*

The most important and significant of the "small" magazines in the Twenties and Thirties was HOUND & HORN. *It published much of the only real critical writing being produced in America at the time, and its interest in the arts was truly catholic. It is no wonder then that in one of its issues—the last before it folded, to be exact, and there was no connection between the two events—*HOUND & HORN *published an article on jazz which is still being discussed today. With a musical scholarship rare in jazz circles, Roger Pryor Dodge investigated the sources of jazz improvisation and linked them with the music of the pre-Bach era. How important and unusual his researches were becomes apparent when it is remembered that in 1934, when* HARPSICHORDS AND JAZZ TRUMPETS *was published, the number of people who had anything more than a hotcha idea of jazz could be numbered on the fingers of one hand. This essay did much for jazz—and unstrangely—for traditional music. Many jazz aficionados turned to the music of Frescobaldi and Corelli, just out of ᴄuriosity, after reading* HARPSICHORDS AND JAZZ TRUMPETS, *and remained to worship. (Ed.)*

IN the history of Jazz we find that the immediate result of the bringing together of the four part hymn and the Negro, was the Spiritual. The Spiritual, though concededly the most original any one thing the Negro has contributed *outright,* seems to me chiefly significant as containing the first seed of Jazz. Unfortunately a great deal more critical interest is expended on the Spiritual out of the *church,* than on the Jazz out of the *dance hall.* In fact, quite aside from my personal conviction that Jazz is by far the most important music of the two, the Spiritual is so well taken care of that new collections are constantly appearing, whereas Jazz, taken for granted as contemporary dance music is scarcely acknowledged, let alone notated. For we can hardly consider a popular song publishing company's issue of the simple Ground Bass, or harmonic vamp accompaniment with occasional uninspired instrumental suggestions, as the written counterpart of that extraordinary and highly developed music. This present lack of adequate notation can be compared very simply to the similar musical situation in Europe during the sixteenth, seventeenth and even eighteenth centuries. In this connection a few lines from a letter written by a certain Andre Maugars in 1639 upon the occasion of a visit to Rome, give an exciting picture of the times:[1]

"I will describe to you the most celebrated and most excellent concert which I have heard . . . As to the instrumental music, it was composed of an organ, a large harpsichord, two or three archlutes, an Archiviole-da-Lyra and two or three violins . . . Now a violin played alone to the organ, then another answered; another time all three played together different parts, then all the instruments went together. Now an archlute made a thousand divisions on ten or twelve notes each of five or six bars length, then the others did the same in a different way. I remember that a violin played in the true chromatic mode and although it seemed harsh to my ear at first, I nevertheless got used to this novelty and took extreme pleasure in it. But above all the great Frescobaldi exhibited thousands of inventions on his harpsichord, the organ always playing the ground. It is not without cause that the famous organist of St. Peter has acquired such a reputation in Europe, for although his published compositions are witnesses to his genius, yet to judge of his profound learning, you must hear him improvise."

He also adds "In the Antienne they had . . . some archlutes playing certain dance tunes and answering one another . . ." (Which, by the way, helps bear out the theory that all great music, even church, leans upon and is developed by the dance.) Now, as then, there is such a

[1] Vide, Arnold Dolmetsch's: *The Interpretations of the Music of the XVIIth and XVIIIth Centuries.*

musical bustle and excitement in the air that no Jazz musician needs more than a harmonic base or a catchy melody, to play extempore in solo or in "consort." Improvised Jazz is comparable to such music as Maugars heard at St. Peters, and though the distorted (to our ears) dynamics and instrumental tone quality of the Negro brass and woodwind sound harsh and fantastic at first, like Maugars, one gets "used to this novelty" and finally takes "extreme pleasure in it." Moreover its start and development occurring during our lifetime, we should feel its power tremendously and have a definite emotional reaction; a purely contemporary enthusiasm, which can never be experienced for a bygone music, no matter how great it was.

When we consider that not only Frescobaldi but Handel, J. S. Bach, Haydn, Mozart and even Beethoven, were all great improvisers, we realize it was intellectual superiority which made them write down what they could improvise more easily—not the limitations of a modern academic composer. We realize that such individuals who could improvise the most difficult and inventive counterpoint and fugue on a keyboard, needed only to push their minds a step further to dispose parts to an orchestra. On the other hand when we consider that the Negro instrumentalist is apparently uninterested and incapable of writing down his own real improvisations, that his inspiration is absolutely dependent upon harmonic progressions provided by other instruments than his own and that though he takes great pleasure in it, his counterpoint is the happy accident of a confrère "getting off" at the same time, then, we can understand perhaps, why this structure of Jazz, this musical development by the instruments themselves (and the different musical styles that implies) is at a standstill as far as native, written composition for solo or symphony goes.

To appreciate the significance of the act of improvisation, we must not overlook the fact that improvisation is absolutely imperative to the development of an art form such as music and dancing. On the other hand we must not overvalue the ability itself, as at the time, this resource must be so commonplace that every performer can avail himself of it with perfect ease. It is when the spirit of a folk school of music so excites the folk artist that it is the most natural thing in the world for him to make variations on every melody he hears, or to invent new melody on a familiar harmony or to extemporize in general, that we find a real freedom of invention. It isn't essential that the whole group experience the same improvisatory spirit. This is the only way, in my opinion, to insure telling change and growth. When this atmosphere does not prevail, the creations of the solitary individual, no matter how revolutionary, always will lack the force of those of a much less important man who has the basic, group impetus back of him. The creations of the former, after the first shock, become more old-fashioned than the most common material of folk improvisation. Richard Wagner is a good example. Moreover it must be understood that by group feeling I do not mean the will to organize a group. A Dalcroze, a Mary Wigman, Les Six or a Picasso may impose rules on a train of satellites, but instead of receiving back new force and inspiration from contemporary fellow artists, on the contrary, they are run into the ground by a coterie of pupils and imitators. Also it must be understood that what passes for improvisatory art in our exclusive little studios of both dancing and music, where the girls and boys find new freedom in expressing the machine-age or the dynamic release of the soul, or in musical combinations in the manner of the written works of Liszt, Scriabin, Milhaud or Gershwin, is not the art of improvisation that 1 discuss.

Whereas the academic child prodigies of today content their masters and their public with nothing more than a mature reading of a score, even a child in early days was expected to improvise, and the quality of his extemporaneous playing was the criterion by which he was judged. When Mozart held an audition for the child Beethoven, he fell half asleep listening to what he presumed were prepared pieces. When Beethoven, greatly vexed, for he had been improvising, insisted the Master give him a theme and then made countless variations on it, Mozart is reported to have jumped up crying, "Pay attention to him: he will make a noise in the world some day." And when Mozart as a child had played for Papa Haydn, he had shown the same prodigal invention. And remember Haydn, Mozart and Beethoven were at the close of a great musical period and were improvising as that tradition had demanded, even though they themselves were the founders of the Romantic Virtuoso movement. It is for that involuntary, impersonal connection with the past that I mention them, not for the new avenue they opened up for the nineteenth century.

If we turn to the musical literature of the seventeenth and eighteenth centuries we find that no two artists were supposed to play identical variations and ornaments on the same piece; on the contrary, the artist was expected extemporaneously to fill in rests, ornament whole notes and rhythmically break up chords. The basic melody, as in Jazz, was considered common property. If the player exactly imitated somebody else or faithfully followed the written compositions of another composer, he was a student, not a professional. However, to the student we owe the inspiring textbooks written by such masters as Couperin, Ph. E. Bach, Geminiani, Mace, Quantz, etc. This is a literature which from all sides presses the fact that if the pupil has no natural inspiration and fantasy in melody, no feeling as to how long to trill, or where to grace notes, or in what rhythm to break up a figured bass, he had better give up all hope of pleasing his contemporaries. It was not the contemporary virtuoso, professional or semi-professional musician who benefited by the few notations in circulation. It was the student. The fact is, that in a healthy school of music it is a drawback to have to read music. It is unnecessary to write it for your own convenience and too much trouble to take the infinite pains necessary to notate a fellow artist's daily compositions. In such a school it is the well balanced composer not depending on written notes himself, but with an eye on posterity or with pupils to interest, who takes the pains to notate more than the simple harmony or melody.

At that time one listened first, as one does now to Jazz, for the melody, then recognized the variations as such and drew intense enjoyment from the musical talent familiarly inspired. Instead of waiting months for a show piece to be composed and then interpreted (our modern academic procedure), then, in one evening, you could hear a thousand beautiful pieces, as you can now in Jazz. Instead of going to a dance hall to hear Armstrong, in earlier times you might have gone to church to hear Frescobaldi; or danced all night to Haydn's orchestra; or attended a salon and listened to Handel accompany a violinist—with his extemporaneous variations so matter of course; or sneaked in on one of Bach's little evenings at home, when to prove his theory of the well-tempered clavier he would improvise in every key, not a stunt improvisation in the manner of someone else, but preludes and fugues probably vastly superior to his famous notated ones. Academicians of today can improvise in the styles of various old schools but the result is commonplace, not only because of the fact of improvising in a school that is out of date, but because such an urge is precious and weak in itself, limiting the improviser to forms he has already seen in print. Even in contemporary modern music, the working out is so intellectual that the extempore act does not give the modernist time to concoct anything he himself would consider significant.

Contrary to the modern academician and similar to the early composers, Jazz musicians give forth a folk utterance, impossible to notate adequately. For even if every little rest, 64th note, slide, trill, mute, blast and rhythmic accent is approximately notated and handed back to them, it is impossible to get them to read it. To read with any facility these extremely difficult improvisations takes a highly developed academic training, a training which is not general, usually, till the best part of an improvising- period is past. The great Negro musicians are not pianists or harpsichordists consciously contrapuntal. The very range of the keyboard which stimulated the seventeenth and eighteenth century European mind to great solo feats of combined polyphonic and harmonic invention only suggests to them, for the most part, a simple harmonic, rhythmic accompaniment. The Negro is par excellence an instrumentalist: a trumpeter, a trombonist, a clarinetist. He is still musically unconscious of what he has done or what he may do. But, do not conclude from this that Jazz music is still at the simple folk-tune stage. Far from it. For though the birth of the Spiritual was the birth of a new folk song containing the seed of Jazz, Jazz itself is something more than just another folk tune. Jazz has reached the highest development of any folk music since the early Christian hymns and dances grew into the most developed contrapuntal music known to history.

To understand even better the source of Jazz, remember the Spiritual is a song, a highly developed hymn if you will, compared to which the Blues, the seed manifestation, is really a step backward in the direction of the Chant: a step altogether natural and necessary for a new art form to take, as witness the retrogression of early Christian music surrounded by Greco-Roman culture. Although the simple sing-song monotonous way of both Blues and Spirituals reveals a lack of depth, comparatively foreign to the old Chant, this is to be explained, I think, by an appreciation of the vast difference in direct antecedents. The Negro received his little bit of the greatness of a Choral, from the Protestant Hymn mixed with Moody and Sankey. Whereas the Gregorian Chant came out of the austere Greek modes mixed with the passionate Semitic plain song. Also, the tunes which skimmed along in the drawing-rooms and music halls during the whole of the nineteenth century, were principally polkas, Irish reels, jigs or the schottische. These the Negro was quite naturally exposed to. So as he was breaking down the four part hymn into the Spiritual, so was he, through his own heritage of *rhythm,* twisting this music of the marches and jigs into first, a cake-walk, later—Ragtime. To play this early American dance music he had to accustom himself to the white man's musical instruments; and it was this familiarization which laid the foundation for his extraordinary instrumental development into Jazz.

Ragtime, we now perceive, was the rhythmical twist the Negro gave to the early American dance tune. Here, the different instruments were finding their places in the musical pattern and already daring to add their own peculiar instrumental qualities. But—suddenly, the whole breadth of melodic and harmonic difference between the folk-tune stuff Ragtime was made out of, and the Chant stuff the racial Blues were made out of, touched something very deep in the Negro. He found himself going way beyond anything he had done so far. For he had now incorporated his own melodic Blues within his own syncopated dance rhythms and miraculously created a new music—a new music which moved him so emotionally that Jazz bands sprang up like mushrooms all around him. The Blues, retrogressed hymn, secular Spiritual, had fathered itself by way of the clarinet, trumpet, trombone, banjo, drums and piano into a rebirth, and christened itself JAZZ!

Now, the many things that go into making a *playing style* suit one instrument rather than another, are usually taken for granted. As a matter of fact they are the result of an experimental development which takes time and is very interesting to trace. The playing style of the harpsichord was not evolved in a day and neither was the playing style of the Jazz valve trumpet. Both started by emulating the human voice (the harpsichord by way of the organ); that is, they took their melody from the singers; and both twisted this song into a stronger instrumental form. Taking these two examples as broadly representative of their respective cultures, we can see of what little importance, after the first vital impulse, the human voice was in the development of these two

musics. I doubt if the voice could ever carry the development of a music
very far without the advent of a composer, as there always seems to be
such satisfaction for a folk singer in repeating verse after verse and letting the words alone be inventive. Though the harpsichord seems a very
complicated instrument to compare alongside the single-noted valve
trumpet, or a slide trombone, nevertheless I feel more of a true basis
of comparison here than with, say, the trumpet and violin. We moderns
only know the present virtuoso violin, an instrument without any real
inventive playing style of its own—an instrument merely swinging
back and forth between the imitative sweet singing of a tune and the
highly developed musical figures lifted out of keyboard music. But a
careful, lively carrying out of all the turns and graces of old music on
the harpsichord, can give us a fairly clear outlook on the playing style
two or three hundred years ago; and only the extreme artificiality of the
harpsichord has made this possible. Any instrument with the dynamic
range of the modern piano and violin, possesses, possibly, a clean crystallized style at the outset, but the traditional playing style can be absolutely
swept away by one little wave of romanticism. The mechanical construction of the harpsichord itself has stood in the way of any such
collapse into smooth and suave decadence.

If in the harpsichord music of the seventeenth and eighteenth centuries we find crystallized the various styles of the other instruments,
it is due to the fact that while that instrument lasted, a fairly traditional
way of playing persisted. Since the birth of the augmented symphonic
orchestra, one hundred years or so ago, we have been listening to luke-
warm instruments, some forgetful of a playing style originally belong-
ing to them and others unaware of a playing style possible to them.
They have no bite in performance. They are completely swamped under
the arbitrary dictum of a conductor reading the arbitrary dictum of a
composer. Such a clever, dramatic juxtaposition of instruments, as
indicated by Stravinsky seems to me no more than clever, and absolutely no more than one man can do without help from the instruments
themselves. And I think, whatever his followers may be still doing, he
himself is aware of this in some sort of a way and feels that he is tired
of exploiting the folk tune, horizontally, vertically, atonally, seriously
or comically. I do not call intellectual messing around with the tone

colors of atrophied, academic conservatory instrumentalists, composition in significant instrumental playing style. And I know, merely intellectually, one could never invent such a style. A *playing style* does not spring out of subjective interpretation or subjective composition. It springs out of primitive group feeling spreading itself deliriously, growing and feeding upon itself. Out of this feeling may or may not appear conscious, composing artists. Their appearance is, however, the beginning of the end, for from then on the group tends towards *listening,* not *participating,* and it is not long before the composer becomes one of a small class, forced to fall back on himself and his kind for nourishment. In this connection consider the most natural of instruments, the human body. In seventeenth and eighteenth century ballet, we know there existed a highly significant and artificial movement and posture. Now we see its complete romantic disintegration—the brief spurt of modern ballet being more of a healthy modernist criticism than actual healthy, artificial dancing. Of the old technique of ballet all we have left is disintegration; and a revolt against disintegration as intellectually manufactured as Schonberg's revolt against harmonic accord.

The shaping of melody by the instruments involved is something I feel accounts not only for the character of old European music but for the character of Jazz; and the development of the latter I have had the opportunity of observing. First, the trumpet, piercing and high pitched, dominating the whole orchestra as it could, took over the principal presentation and variations of the melody, something hitherto left to the violins. So the importance of the first violinist vanished, the first trumpeter taking his place. In a limited way the trumpeter already held this position in the military brass band, but there he was either traditional *cor de chasse, cor de bataille* or simply playing violin or voice music relegated to the trumpet. In a Jazz orchestra he is inventing his own music and doing things previously considered impossible on such an instrument. In order to satisfy a wild desire to play higher and higher he blew harder and harder and in the process made unavoidable squawks and fouled notes. These not only surprised but delighted him, and now, though he has a trumpet technique inferior to none, he still blasts and blows foul notes in beautiful and subtle succession, and with his extraordinary manipulation of mutes gets a hushed dramatic intensity that entails harder blowing than ever before. This difficulty of performance has kept the trumpet, so far, melodically inventive in the hands of the inventors, plus a few white imitators. But lately even the great artist, Louis Armstrong, has fallen into a florid cadenza style, induced, I fear, by excess technical ease. Armstrong has always favored the "open" manner of trumpet playing and a melody of the wide, broken chord variety, seemingly impossible in range. Even when he sings he is really playing trumpet solos with his voice.

The natural playing style of the slide trombone quite obviously would be dictated by the rhythmic movement of the arm sliding back and forth, something no trombonist has been allowed to feel heretofore. The Negro trombone player has become a sort of dancer in the rhythmic play of his right arm. He makes this instrument live, by improvising solos as natural to a trombone as the simplest of folk tunes are to the voice. This cannot be said of the trombone in any other music save Jazz. However, as important as this instrument is, I find because of its low register and a certain cumbersomeness in size, that the trumpet has gone beyond it in inventiveness, even carrying further the trombone's own newly created rhythmic and melodic twists. This copying of one another's style we meet constantly, and in order not to detract from the original creative importance I wish to distribute amongst the various instruments, it is well to understand how that which one instrument creates another may incorporate to more complete advantage. In other words, many trumpets can play in trombone style but I've heard only one trombonist create trumpet melodies, and he is Joseph Nanton (Tricky Sam) of Duke Ellington's orchestra. Theirs is a lazy style, which the trumpeter has seized upon with the rhythmic instinct of his mind and transposed to the trumpet for variety's sake, but which they, having conceived, are confined to. At this stage of the game if we had to choose between trumpet and trombone we would find the trumpet more of an all around instrument.

The faculty of imitation is possessed to a high degree by the pianist and almost to the exclusion of originality. This of course has not tended to make him an important contributing factor to Jazz. The piano has been pretty generally relegated to the position of harmonic and rhythmic background and its occasional excursions into the foreground are not noticeably happy in inspiration. Owing to the conspicuous common-placeness of our virtuosi, the Negro pianist only too easily slips into the fluid superficialities of a Liszt cadenza.[2] This tendency of the Negro to imitate the florid piano music of the 19th century which he hears all around him, has kept the piano backward in finding its own Jazz medium. It takes a very developed musical sense to improvise significantly on the piano; a talent for thinking in more than one voice. The counterpoint that Jazz instruments achieve ensemble is possible to a certain extent on the piano alone, but this takes a degree of development Jazz has not yet reached. The best piano solos so far, in my opinion, are the melodic "breaks" imitating trumpet and trombone. Lately the pianist has found some biting chords, and felt a new desire to break up melody, not only rhythmically as inspired by the drum, but rhythmically as a percussion instrument fundamentally inspired by its own peculiar harmonic percussion. This perhaps, will lead him to contribute something no other musician has. Claude Hopkins is a notable example of such a pianist, but on the other hand Bix Beiderbecke (white) is doing this, and seems to have lost all sense of melody in the process. His intellect has gone ahead of his emotion, instead of keeping pace with it. That is the main trouble I find with our "hot" white orchestras. All they have they got from the Negro, and they are a little too inclined to fling back the word "corny." Until their own output proves more truly melodic or the Negro has completely succumbed to the surrounding decadence, they are still melodically "catching up" to the Negro.

The clarinet has been the instrument of very inventive players but somehow its facile technique has inspired florid rippling solos only too often. The saxophones have found their place, playing the background harmony in threes and taking the "sweet" choruses. Though I dislike the way the saxophone is generally played, it can be as "hot" as the clarinet when it is "jazzed up"; however, it is mostly used for soft, sentimental passages. The drums on occasion have qualified the playing style of the entire orchestra, as in the old washboard bands. Nobody who has heard a clarinetist used to playing in conjunction with a washboard, can have missed noticing the persistently syncopated and gallop-

[2] Dodge had at this time obviously not discovered boogie-woogie piano (Ed.)

ing style induced by the incessant rubadubadubadub of the washboard. Amazing things have been done with kettle drums, and any good drummer can take a "break" and off-hand crowd into it more exciting rhythms than a Modernist can concoct after the lengthiest meditation. The violin has not been favored by the hot Jazz bands although when "jazzed up" it falls in very readily with the spirit. Here again we can see the same musical result of the arm movement as in the case of the trombone, although not quite as pronounced. The style of playing, I should judge, is similar to that in vogue before the advent of the tight bow. They even get an effect of the old bow by loosening the hair and wedging the violin in between the hair and the bow and then playing all the strings of the violin at once. The remaining instruments, bass fiddle, guitar, banjo and tuba are in very versatile hands but for the most part contribute solos in styles similar to the ones I have already discussed. They have contributed, however, a few individual elements such as the "slap" of the bass or the contrapuntal, inventive accompaniment of the guitar.

A Jazz composition is made up of the improvisations of these players, and although the arranger is coming more and more into prominence, his work is still very secondary. The arranger takes a fragmentary rhythm from an improvisation on a given melody, and applies this rhythm over and over again throughout the natural course of the melody. Maybe this rhythm is given to the three trumpets, and a counter theme given to the other musicians; but in any case it is usually musically very uninteresting and only saved by the piercing interpretation of the men in the better bands. Though most written music of Moderato Tempo or faster, from Haydn on, has had such rhythmic patterns applied throughout, the composers have been conscious of their best melodic phrases and have woven them into the piece with intellectual skill. But this being one of the last stages in folk development, the Jazz arrangers are not equal to the task and their output is very tiresome. Even if any highly inventive improvisation should be orchestrated into the score it would lose its original appeal through the selfconsciousness of the reader, for the actual melodic richness is unappreciated both by the Jazz player as well as the listeners, only the robust playing style of the instrumentalist exciting their admiration.

It is a fact that the many Jazz orchestras playing under the name of a star performer or leader, mislead the public into thinking that the leader or performer creates the music. This brings up the question as to how we should rate benefactors, managers, impresarios and the like, of all large organizations promoting art, whether opera, ballet, symphony or Jazz orchestra. The Diaghileff Ballets are a good example, for these productions included not only the dancers and choreographers, painters and musicians, but Diaghileff, upon whom depended everything from the securing of backing to the choice of ballets. He managed the financing, he controlled and selected the great artists, smoothing out their differences, and he proved himself a rare man; probably more rare than any single one of the artists. But important as he was to the life of the organization, students will always pick out the important separate creators and give them their due credit, for these were the people who were the backbone of the organization and upon whom all lasting significance depends. To attribute their art significance to Diaghileff is as foolish as it would be to attribute a Beethoven Symphony to any one of his benefactors. I think the Jazz orchestra is placed in about the same situation. There are players, arrangers and a personality in every orchestra, and the leader can be anything from the best player to no practicing musician at all. He can be everything from a great personality to a shrewd business man, and whether he is a musician or not he is always able to take the role of a master of ceremonies. He usually sets the policy of the orchestra, and is responsible for the quality of players and arrangements. Also we find the leader, more often than not, employs orchestrators. As a rule he *can* orchestrate, but because of the tiresome routine of public performance and the running of the organization, he employs, let us say, the saxophonist to do this tedious job, though since all except a few pieces are simply arrangements of passing popular tunes, any outsider does just as well. When we see the names of two composers on a piece of music, one well known and the other unknown, we can guess who did the composing. Always look for this other name before attributing the work to the well known name. And of course on a record of this piece where the melody is entirely changed into a new vastly more important synthesis by an unknown individual in the orchestra, we see only the name of the original composer, as no musical importance is attached to these variations. In Jazz as in Ballet, the public must discover for itself who is responsible for the various works.

The four solos that follow are notated from records made by Bubber Miley. He said they were variations on a Spiritual his mother used to sing, called *Hosanna,* but the Spiritual turns out to be a part of Stephen Adams' *Holy City* commencing at the seventeenth bar. There the tune is in four-four time and eight bars long, but Miley's version has but

BLACK AND TAN FANTASY

Fig.1.

BUBBER MILEY

two bars taken out next to the last bar and the remaining six bars drawn out to twelve by dividing each bar into two. In the composition *Black and Tan Fantasy* this theme is announced in the minor, but his hot solos (variations) are on the original major. As he improvises these solos the orchestra simply plays a "vamp" rhythmic accompaniment. I have written them out under each other as in an orchestral score, with the theme on top, in order to facilitate intercomparison; but it must be understood that these are pure improvisations out of a folk school, with

Fig. 2

no idea of adequate notation. All of these solos are by Bubber Miley except the first twelve bars of No. 2 which is by Joseph Nanton, a trombonist in Duke Ellington's orchestra. As I have said, Negro improvisations are either on the melody or on the harmony, and it would appear that Miley paid no attention to the melody, so far removed are his variations; but by playing certain parts of the theme, then the corresponding part in any one of the hot solos, you will find that many times he did have the theme in mind.

In No. 1, all through the first twelve bars, there is a vague resemblance to the theme. The thirteenth and fifteenth bars are exactly the same as the theme but his treatment of these bars takes the startling form of blasts. In No. 3, if we play the fifth and sixth bars of the theme, and then his corresponding variations, we again see a melodic resemblance, but it is curious how this is his first melodic attack after the four bar hold; that is, instead of continuing with the melody, he is starting one.

In the thirteenth bar of No. 3 he wonderfully distorts the B flat in the theme, to an E natural. Here is a take off of the most extreme kind, and accordingly he followed the harmony until he could catch up with the melody. This he did at the twenty-first bar, finishing with a jazzed up version of the theme.

A typical Jazz distortion of the given melody is to lengthen the time value of one note by stealing from another, thereby sometimes reducing the melody to an organ point. Though this was practiced prior to Miley, it is interesting to see how the whole note in the first bar of the theme is held longer and longer until in No. 4 he is holding it seven bars. Notice how the improvisations do not have any break between the twelfth and thirteenth bars, that is, where the theme begins its repeat.

It seems to me the little phrases in bars eight, nine and ten of No. 1, where he plays with his melody at either end of the octave, can only be found elsewhere in such music as Bach's *Goldberg Variations*. For example:

Fig. 3.   J.S. BACH

Joseph Nanton's twelve bar variation in No. 2 seems to be on the harmony. It is followed by Miley's beautiful entrance, a slow trill on the original B flat. In No. 4, which he made for me, the little coda to the long note is the purest music I have ever heard in Jazz. I speak of purity in its resemblance to the opening of the Credo for soprano voices in Palestrina's *Missa Papae Marcelli.* You will observe that the thirteenth bars of both No. 3 and No. 4 are the same. The freedom leading up to the C in the fifteenth bar is amazing and the A flat in the nineteenth bar, after all the agitation, is no less surprising.

Fig. 4.   PALESTRINA

There were two elements essential for this freedom of thought; harmony and rhythm. Miley told me he needed the strictest beat and at least a three part harmony. Though the piano could give him this, he was always better, however, with the orchestra and its background of drums, etc. Whereas the academy now might be able to compose parts like this, write them down and with a little shaping make something very inventive, no folk artist could do so, as his improvising in such a manner that rhythm and melody are torn apart, really demands these two elements. We can now understand how a person like Duke Ellington was indispensable to Miley—"When I get off the Duke is always there." The Duke's cooperation, in fact, inspired Miley to the best work he ever did and neither of them sustained very well their unfortunate parting of the ways. The Duke has never since touched the heights that he and Bubber Miley reached in such records as *East St. Louis Toodle-O, Flaming Youth, Got Everything But You, Yellow Dog Blues,* etc., etc.—and of course the many *Black and Tan Fantasies.* The sudden and tragic death of Bubber Miley put a stop to his career before he was thirty—though without the guidance of the Duke, who is a real Diaghileff in a small way, perhaps he would have slipped backwards too.

In an article I wrote seven years ago entitled "Negro Jazz" I held out high hopes for the art, though at the time those critics who deigned to notice Jazz were in no undecided terms announcing its complete extinction. Since that time Jazz has not only persisted but advanced way beyond my expectations. It is only now that I have my doubts; it is the present tendencies that seem to be spelling doom in the near future. For the Negro is tired of the Blues and likes to write the popular tunes which are a sort of compromise between his former music and Tin-Pan Alley, and fairly eats up any like compromise of a white person. There are few real Blues singers left like Bessie Smith. Her inventive way of singing does not seem to have been contagious. When I hear an early record of Bessie Smith's and then listen to a Cab Calloway and see how much more the Negro now enjoys the latter, I realize that the Blues have been superseded and white decadence has once more ironed out and sweetened a vital art. At the moment, through the arrangers and the more conscious players, Jazz is in process of being crystallized into a written music, but the gulf is too great between this and what I consider good Jazz, for such a crystallization to have any significance in the future.

One would suppose that academic composers would jump at this medium, but the little that has been done in the field is of less value than those arrangements I have spoken of. With the awareness of an academic education, the composers have combined the simple side of Jazz with the complex side of modern music and the public, with a similar viewpoint towards the treatment of such music, finds it interesting. But even for them this music does not seem to wear well and probably is no more than their standard of novelty. Our composers may have the craftsmanship of Bach still sticking in their craws, but they lack even a taste of his melodic significance—it is an already embellished melody of the seventeenth and eighteenth centuries which Bach has so vitally mixed with his craftsmanship. These Moderns give us musical mathematics and acrobatics applied to any and every folk tune, but their work lacks as true a line of melody as we might find in the most obscure trombone solo. As I am in complete accord with other Moderns who theoretically object to using Jazz, it must be understood that I am not urging composers to *use* it in the same sense that Dvorak *used* folk tunes. What I propose for consideration is, that as this whole period is permeated with Jazz, it cannot be such a precious or out-of-the-way attitude to become *part of it*. Though a fine Modern-Jazz music may still be written, frankly, the best I think we can hope for is that this eating decadence of Jazz be a slow process, and that in the meantime the Negro will crystallize more of his work on records, such work as Duke Ellington and Bubber Miley turned out in the old days.

Of the many American writings on Jazz, both pro and con, few are knowledgeably critical, none of any instructive value. There are magazines and articles in Europe with an attitude towards Jazz as serious music, that we haven't approached. And there is Prunières, the one important critic, to my knowledge, who has an appreciation of the improvised solo in Jazz. The American criticisms on the subject seem confusedly to hover around on the one hand, the spirit of America, the brave tempo of modern life, absence of sentimentalism, the importance of syncopation and the good old Virginia cornfields; and on the other hand, the monotonous beat, the unmusical noises, the jaded Harlem Negro, alcoholism and sexual debauch. These solos in the *Black and Tan Fantasy* may not have the significance I attribute to them but they could at least be a premise for criticism. As notated music it certainly is not just noise, squawks and monotonous rhythm: nor do vague favorable praises seem appropriate. Such solos as I have printed, demand musical investigation.

The Blues

ABBÉ NILES
from *The Blues,* by W. C. Handy

This essay on the blues, published in 1926 as an introduction to a collection of W. C. Handy pieces, was the first contact many people had with the lore and the history of jazz. It must have been an eye-opener to people fed on the Whiteman-King-of-Jazz pap. Even today, Abbé Niles' study is still crammed full of interesting information and data for the jazz historian and the jazz musicologist. That it is also given to misapprehensions will be obvious to any student of hot music, but even these lacks are of interest today for they show just how far research into the nature of jazz and the blues have gone in the twenty years since Niles published his essay.

Roger Pryor Dodge, in his analysis of the critics written for Jazzmen, considered the Niles introduction and the Handy collection a "very important book" which "demonstrates the usual confusion of a critic when faced with the first extension of a new folk form," and finds Niles "by far most competent when analyzing the actual blues." When one recalls that Niles was starting from scratch, and bucking the trend of adulation for "symphonic jazz" as the last word, the value of his contribution and the astuteness of his insight become apparent. (ED.)

THE blues sprang up among illiterate and more or less despised classes of Southern Negroes: barroom pianists, careless nomadic laborers, watchers of incoming trains and steamboats, street-corner guitar players, strumpets and outcasts. A spiritual is matter for choral treatment; a blues was a one-man affair, originating typically as the expression of the singer's feelings, and complete in a single verse. It might start as little more than an interjection, a single line; sung, because singing was as natural a method of expression as speaking. But while the idea might be developed, if at all, in any one of many forms of songs, there was one which, perhaps through its very simplicity and suitability for improvisation, became very popular: the line would be sung, repeated, repeated once again; with the second repetition some inner voice would say "enough," and there would have come into being a crude blues:

> *Gwine take morphine an' die,*
> *Gwine take morphine an' die,*
> *Gwine take morphine an' die.*

Its air might be new, but by no means need be; under various names the old three-line song, *Joe Turner,*[1] was known and sung by Negroes all over the South, and to its tune, if to no other familiar, the impromptu could be fitted; the tune, indeed, might help in framing the words; better yet, with that tune there might be associated already various other verses, plaintive, smart or obscene, which the singer might tack on after speaking his own mind. If his conceit had merit, it would be gladly adopted by its hearers, if any; had his tune a melodic or rhythmical twist of its own, his words might be forgotten, but the air pass around as a vehicle for the old expressions, common property of the race, which would without difficulty be fitted to it.[2]

The thought would not necessarily be expressed in a single line, twice repeated without variation. There might be and usually was one repetition, but instead, the second line might slightly modify, by way of emphasis, the first,[3] while the third would introduce something new: lines one and two having expressed, say, some grief, wistful reflection, or some unhopeful "if," line three would now supply a reason for the grief, some collateral conclusion, or the course which would be taken should the "if" come true; the third thus became the important line, releasing the tension accumulated during the repetition of the first:

---

[1] Published in the collection. (ED.)

[2] But few individual blues tunes seem to have had a wide currency.

[3] This slight modification was matter of individual choice, and is shown in few of the examples given here.

Gwine lay my head right on de railroad track,
Gwine lay my head right on de railroad track,
'Cause my baby, she won't take me back.

Gwine lay my head right on de railroad track,
Gwine lay my head right on de railroad track,
If de train come 'long, I'm gwine to snatch it back.

Don't want no man puttin' sugar in my tea,
Don't want no man puttin' sugar in my tea,
'Cause I'm evil,⁴ 'fraid he might poison me.

If I had wings, like Nora's ⁵ faithful dove,—
Had strong wings, like Nora's faithful dove,
I would fly away, to de man I love.

Depression, while the most common motive of the blues verses, is
not universal. They may give some shrewd general comment, for
which their epigrammatic form is well adapted:

Ketch two women runnin' togedder long,
Ketch two women runnin' togedder long,
You can bet yo' life dere's somethin' gwine wrong.

If yo' house ketch fire, and dey ain't no water roun',
If yo' house ketch fire, and dey ain't no water roun',
Throw yo' trunk out de window, an' let de shack buhn down.⁶

The spirit may be of ridicule:

Dey's two kind of people in dis worl', dat I can't stan',
Dey's two kind of people in dis worl', dat I can't stan',
An' dat's a two-faced woman, an' a monkey-man.⁷

The modern published songs run to the theme of love, and some of the
folk-blues were love-songs:

⁴ *i. e.,* have a bad conscience or reputation.
⁵ Noah's.
⁶ From the point of view of the Southern small town Negro this was wisdom. If it started,
it usually did burn down, for all the fire-department cared.
⁷ Afro-American epithet for a West Indian.

When you see me comin', h'ist yo' window high,
When you see me comin', h'ist yo' window high,
When you see me goin', hang yo' head an' cry.[8]

Oh, de Mississippi River is so deep an' wide
Oh, de Mississippi River is so deep an' wide
An' my gal lives on de odder side.

Oh, de Kate's up de river, Stack is in de ben',
Oh, de Kate's up de river, Stack is in de ben',
And I ain't seen my baby since I don' know when.[9]

There is the motive of longing to be elsewhere, as in the crude

Gwine down de river befo' long,
Gwine down de river befo' long,
Gwine down de river befo' long,

and as in the following, which was sung (of all places) in Texas:

Michigan water tastes like sherry wine,
Michigan water tastes like sherry wine,
I'm gwine back to Michigan, to de one I lef' behin'.

Here is an unassorted collection:

Boll-weevil, where you been so long?
Boll-weevil, where you been so long?
You stole my cotton, now you wants my cohn.

Boll-weevil, don't you sing de blues no mo',
Boll-weevil, don't you sing de blues no mo',
Boll-weevil's everywhere you go.[10]

B'lieve to my soul, dat man's got a black cat's bone.
(I said black-cat; I mean bone.)

[8] The last five words constitute a favorite phrase, found in many of the folk songs.
[9] The reference is to the Mississippi River steamboats Kate Adams and Stackolee, of the Lee Line, and dates the verse back twenty years or more. The singer should be pictured lying under a tree on the river-bank and recognizing the two whistles.
[10] The boll-weevil, which inspired one of the most famous folksongs, is a symbol for all petty gougers and "cutters." In Mississippi he lent his name to the railroad conductors.

B'lieve to my soul, dat man's got a black cat's bone.
(I said black-cat; I mean bone.)
Every time I leave him, I got to hurry back home.[11]

Let me be yo' rag-doll till yo' tidy [12] *come,*
If he can beat me raggin', he's got to rag it some,—my honey
How *long has I got to wait?*
Oh, can I git you now, or must I hesitate?

Ashes to ashes, an' a-dus' to dus',
Ef de whisky don't git you, den de cocaine mus',—my honey, etc.

Did you ever see yo' honey, when her good man's not aroun'?
Did you ever see yo' honey, when her good man's not aroun'?
She gets up in de mo'nin', tuhns de feader-bed upside-down.[13]

If you want to keep yo' baby, better git yo'self a lock an' key,
If you want to keep yo' baby, better git yo'self a lock an' key,
'Cause too many men a-been stealin' my baby from me.[13]

My moder's dead, my fader's 'crost de sea,
My moder's dead, my fader's 'crost de sea,
Ain't got nobody to feel an' care for me.[14]

Gwine to de river, take a rockin' chair,
Gwine to de river, take a rockin' chair,
If de blues o'ertake me, gwine rock 'way from dere.[15]

[11] A song of jealousy. A black cat's bone is the equivalent of a rabbit's foot, and valuable in love.

[12] This and the following represent two great series of verses sung to "Must I Hesitate" or to the first part of "Hesitating Blues," each to the same refrain. Most of them are too powerful for these pages. The first two lines are sung as one, *i. e.*, they occupy the same number of bars as each of the two lines of the refrain. This may be the only blues with a refrain. "Tidy" is the dressed-up official lover, the "steady."

[13] Supplied by Langston Hughes, author of "The Weary Blues."

[14] From Mississippi. A former if not present frequency of illicit affairs between Negroes and foreign-born whites, and even marriages of Negroes with Chinese, in this region, makes the verse more plausible than it appears at first sight.

[15] There are many of these "gwine to de river" verses, and cf. Handy's "Beale Street Blues"

> Going to the river, maybe, by-and-by,
> Going to the river, and there's a reason why,—
> Because the river is wet, and Beale Street's done gone dry.

Gwine to de river, take a rope an' a rock,
Gwine to de river, take a rope an' a rock,
Gwine to tie rope roun' my neck, an' jump right over de dock.[16]

Got full o' my moonshine, walked de streets all night,
Got full o' my moonshine, walked de streets all night,
Squabblin' wid my black gal, 'cause she wasn't white.

  If I could holler like a mountin' jack,
  If I could holler like a mountin' jack,
  I'd go up on de hillside, an' call my rider back.[17]

The scope of the blues verses is so wide that one might almost expect to run on a stanza expressing solid satisfaction. Without knowledge of such a verse claiming folk-lore origin, one may cite Handy's words to that chant of subterranean contentment, *Basement Blues,* as quoted hereafter at page 55. Not melancholy, but the singer's personality, is the most universally conspicuous element. In almost every case whatever is said is in some way brought back to *him;* he deals in his troubles, his opinions of life and people, his resentments, his desires, and there seems to be room left for his pleasures. If it be suggested that even in a mere saw such as "If yo' house buhn down," there is Melancholy in the Miltonian sense, what is to be made of the invincible optimism of:

What you gwine to do when dey buhn de bar'l-house down?
What you gwine to do when dey buhn de bar'l-house down?
Gwine move out de piano, an' bar'l-house on de groun'.

But most of such verses are in a spirit which would make it appropriate to call them "blue" taken by themselves; and it is a safe guess that this accounts for the name bestowed on the tunes to which they were sung.

The very essence of the majority, indeed, is found in the traditional line, common property of the race:

[16] Supplied by Walter F. White, author of "The Fire in the Flint" and "Flight."
[17] "Jack" is "jackass." "Rider," "easy rider," which term means both lover and (not either, or) procurer. In this case the emphasis is on the former aspect of the word. Fidelity to his woman is expected of the easy rider under the inverted single standard of morality on which their home is founded; the classic example is the song "Frankie and Johnny."

Got de blues, but too dam' mean to cry.

What makes the typical words, as well as the music, striking,—what
has caught the attention of white song writers who were indifferent to
the musical devices by which it was expressed,—is an unconscious
philosophy between the lines, of making a little mirth of one's troubles
while one dwells on them; of choosing as the reaction to disaster,
laughter instead of tears; instead of sodden despondency, an attrac-
tively unexpected mood, exuberant and fantastic, native, not virtu-
ously forced, finding a gusto in its self-expression. Just to show how
plain unlucky she is, says she:

> *Went to de gypsy, to have my fortune tol',*
> *Went to de gypsy, to have my fortune tol',—*
> *Gypsy tol' me, doggone you, girlie, doggone yo' bad-luck soul.*

And for another perfect example of the spirit:

> *De brook run into de river, river run into de sea,*
> *De brook run into de river, river run into de sea,—*
> *An' if I don't run into my daddy, paw's gwine have to bury me.*

Yet another is supplied by Handy, the impromptu remark, overheard
by him, of a Memphis mule-driver:

> "G'wan, Mule!
> *Don't you want to wuhk?*
>
> *Hadn't ought t'been a mule.*
> *Ought t' been a woman.*
> *Then I'd be wuhkin' fo' you.*
> G'wan, Mule!"

A logical objection will occur to the exclusion of verse not in the three-
line form. It is quite true that very many verses not in this form are
found in the folk-lore which are in the blues spirit; indeed, that the
sense of the examples cited here can always be expressed in a couplet.
To this, it may be answered that it was the verses which could be fitted

into the blues tunes, that came by that token to be called blues; while, working in a circle, the Memphis Negroes in the middle of the last decade would say of a new air to which they could not sing one of their three-line verses: "Dat ain't no blues!"

Structure

THE structural peculiarities of the blues tunes may be the result of those of the stanza, more likely the reverse is the case, but suffice it to say that the blues architecture is admirably adapted to impromptu song and versification alike. Just as the stanza had three lines instead of the two or four normal to simple verse, so the voice would sing (always in two-four or common time) twelve instead of the normal eight or sixteen bars to the strain, each line being complete in four bars of the air. As each line usually expressed a thought which, with a period after it, would still make sense, so the air with the last syllable of each line would return to the keynote or the tonic third or fifth, so that the whole presented a period of three semi-independent phrases,—three wing-clipped hops (separated, as will be shown, by noticeable intervals) instead of one sustained flight—with successive bizarre effects of internal finality and of final incompleteness. Where one expects the melody to stop it resumes; just as one is waiting for a fourth, and final, phrase, it stops, and instinct calls for a repetition. Take the classic, *Joe Turner:*

JOE TURNER

Dey tell me Joe Tur-ner's come and gone   Dey tell me Joe
Tur-ner's come and gone   Got my man an' gone.

Certain modern examples seem to show a deviation: the first eight bars present a single period with thesis and antithesis, while the last four come in with a coda based on the four preceding. The finding of such a construction in a folk-tune would suggest that in the verse originally sung to it the first two lines expressed a single thought without repetition. What has been done is that the break between the first phrase and

the second has been bridged over. Thus in one of the most beautiful of
blues: [18]

Oh, de Mississippi River, is so deep an'—so wide an' deep, an', so deep
   an' wide, an'—
*De Mississippi River am so deep an' wide
An' de lights buhn low, on de uder side.*

Did you ever wake up in de middle of de night with de blues all round
   you, de blues all round you, did you

[18] Copyright, by McKinley Music Company; copyright assigned (1925) to, and song reprinted by permission of, Triangle Music Company, whose up-to-date version appears as
Dallas Blues. Accompaniment new. Air and words as first heard by the writer in an English
public-house,—but in American accents, and to a ukulele.

Ever wake up with de blues all round yo' bed?
An' no one near, to soothe yo' achin' head?

Oh, de graveyard is a nasty ol' place, dey spade you under, spade you
*   under, dey*
Shovel you under, an' dey throw dirt in yo' face;
Ooh, de graveyard, is a nasty ol' place.

If it be realized that in this song the words in italics are merely "patter," and, like the notes accompanying them, superfluous, it will be seen that the only irregularity is in the short rest between the words "mallard" and "I said," and that if there be inserted in place of this rest the word "duck," to A-flat, the air and verse will be conformed to type. In the well-known *Frankie and Johnny* (a ballad rather than a blues but having a twelve-bar air) the second phrase is bridged to both the first and the third.

In the example first given it will be noted that each line of the words occupies considerably less than its allotted four bars, leaving a long wait before the next sentence and phrase begin. This is typical, and important. It affords to the improviser, for one thing, a space in which his next idea may go through its period of gestation,—and thus is important to him. But to us it is of far greater interest that, assuming he isn't compelled to concentrate on what is to follow, he can utilize this space, not as a hold, but as a *play-ground* in which his voice or instrument may be allowed to wander in such fantastic musical paths as he pleases, returning (not necessarily but usually) to the key-note, third, or fifth, yet again before vacation is over. Regularly in folk-blues the last syllable of each line thus coincides, not only with the keynote or another element of the tonic major triad, *but with the first beat, third bar, of its corresponding four bars of music,* leaving seven quick beats or three slow ones (according to the time-signature) before the melody proper resumes its motion. The irregular rest in *If de River Was Whisky* falls on this crucial beat; the notes which have been characterized as surplusage, and which follow this rest, fill in the following break, and themselves are called "the break," or "the jazz." That example, however, is so concealed and woven into the main frame-work that it will be well to show, with its "breaks," a blues already given *simpliciter:*

JOE TURNER *(2nd Verse)*

He come wid   fo'- ty links of chain   *Oh*   *Lawd-y*   Come wid

fo'- ty links of chain   *Oh*   *Lawd-y*   Got my man an'   gone.

In the folk-blues, the "breaks" or "the jazz" had no such name and were generally as simple as in the specimen last shown and as those in *Got No Mo' Home Than a Dawg;* but there might also be esoteric operations on the banjo or piano, if any, even though the voice merely held through. It is unfortunate that actual transcriptions of these instrumental efforts are lacking; like the songs themselves they were, of course, unwritten, while unlike the songs they could not pass by word of mouth and were not apt to be imitated. One purely improvised instrumental jazz has been preserved, however, namely, the much imitated device in shifting rhythms in the latter part of *Memphis Blues,* which was played by Paul Wyer, violinist in Handy's Memphis Band three years before publication of the song.

Harmony

Unwritten tunes and not normally sung as part songs, these were nevertheless unconsciously so constructed that if the singer wished to accompany himself, he need know only three chords,—the common chords on the keynote and subdominant and the chord of the dominant seventh. (As an example, blues in Handy Collection have been so arranged.) This, though a characteristic common to the type is, on the other hand, by no means peculiar to it; *Swanee River, Yankee Doodle* or *Heilige Nacht* (to mention three out of probable thousands) may be sung to the same three chords.

The Tunes

The melody would consist of three brief phrases, favoring a syncopated jugglery of a very few notes,—often, though not necessarily, those of the pentatonic scale; [19] thus confined is the song *Joe Turner* (disregarding the minor third). The frequent return to the keynote gave an almost hypnotic effect, and the only equally favored note was the tonic third; a fact of the first importance to the blues because of a tendency of the untrained Negro voice when singing the latter tone at an important point, to *worry* it, slurring or wavering between flat and natural. Even in singing to the banjo—a cheerful instrument—the slur might be expected; if to the guitar (the strings of which are normally so arranged as to invite the use of minor chords), it might be even more prominent and would actually be duplicated on the instrument. The explanation for this peculiarity would seem to be furnished by the characteristic fondness for the flatted *seventh,*—and a feeling for the key of the subdominant; of which the tonic third itself *is* the seventh. Reaching the favorite tonic third, perhaps the Afro-American feels it as at such *and* as the seventh of the subdominant, resulting in the flatting, slurring or wavering effect which has been mentioned; to test the theory, experiment on songs in the Handy collection, striking with each rhythmically prominent minor third its seventh below. But to the white listener, thinking in terms of a single scale, this momentary change of key might not be apparent; instead, in view of the importance of the tonic third as an index to mode, the melody, if sung unaccompanied, might seem difficult to classify as either major or minor.

The Name

Though the popularity of the blues form is probably of comparatively recent date, it preceded the name and called it forth. These songs were woven of the same stuff as the other overlapping items in the long list,— the work-songs, love-songs, devil-songs, the over-and-overs, slow-drags, pats, and stomps, yes, and decidedly the spirituals; they were called by

[19] The pentatonic scale omits the tonic fourth and seventh, and so runs "do, re, mi, sol, la." The seeming inappropriateness to pentatonic melodies, of the characteristic accompaniment with its subdominant modulations, is explained on acceptance of Ballanta's theory that the African, despite his frequent singing in this scale, does so without feeling it *as* a scale.

several of these names, and it was not till shortly before 1910 that from
quarters unknown they first received the title "The Blues." By that date
the term in its new sense was known to lower-class Negroes, here and
there, from Missouri and Kentucky down to the Delta. The songs—
independent verses, be it remembered—had no titles to distinguish them
one from another except for their first lines. It has been suggested that
Weary Blues, Worried Blues and the like were merely generic terms,
amplifications of the shorter one; the common impression to the contrary would be shaken if one imagined the white man saying, "What's
that terrible thing you're singing?" and the answer: "Oh, dat's just de
weary blues." And there would be reason in the answer: the blues
were much more a convenient (because very definite) *form* than anything else, so rigid and constricted, that it could serve its purpose as a
vehicle for the common-property verses; of such a character (as already
noted) as to facilitate the improvisation of more. It is quite likely, further
that the folk-song *Joe Turner* is the grandfather of them all. The
original blues may all, till some conscious imitator came in, have been
(so far as the tunes went) conscientious renditions of *Joe Turner* to
the best of the singers' memories; any, because all, then, would have
been simply *The Blues*. With the framework and harmonic scheme
of *Joe Turner* everywhere familiar and perhaps inherently reasonable
and natural to the Negro mind, it might also be adopted quite unconsciously for impromptu melodizing; the improvised melody (generally
of the crudest) might entail so little creative effort that it would be forgotten as soon as sung; the form, however, being built of more durable
stuff, would still stand, ready to be hung with the next flimsy garment,
and the next.[20]

The "Blue Note"

Writing down his tunes with the memory of how the Negroes had
sung, Handy was first met by the problem of perpetuating the typical
treatment of the tonic third,—the slur of the voices, whatever the song.
This aberration he chose to represent by the frequent introduction of
the minor third into melodies which (however melancholy their under-
current) exhibited a prevailing major. It might divide a beat between

[20] Part III of this study of the Blues was a biographical sketch of W. C. Handy, omitted
here, hence the skip in footnote numbers which follows. (ED.)

itself and the major third, appear (more nearly as in the originals) as a grace-note to the major, or here and there entirely replace the major. Handy's interpolated minor third, appearing thus as signifying a change of mode followed by a re-exchange, and appearing nearly as often as the melody reaches the third at all, caught and holds popular attention as have none of the structural peculiarities which alone distinguished the folk-blues from all other Negro song. It has acquired a name of its own: "the blue note." The more of such notes, the "meaner" the blues. Its occasional use furnishes the work of most of the white writers with its only claim (from the historical standpoint) to such titles as *The ———— Blues,* while from the standpoint of the folklorist *Rhapsody In Blue* presents a neat contradiction in terms. It is, in short, a method consciously chosen by W. C. Handy to represent a characteristic vocal treatment of songs *in general* that had impressed him, which has become to most observers the earmark of the blues.

True it is, on the other hand, that it is too late for pedants; for present-day purposes the definition must be expanded. Mr. Virgil Thomson (in *The American Mercury* for August, 1924) refers to "the blues formula,—subdominant modulation with alternations of tonic major and minor"; a definition as correct, so far as it goes, as it is succinct—if one does not look too far back—and which therefore needs to be supplemented rather than seriously quarreled with. Two different things are to be defined, two definitions are called for. And for *Rhapsody in Blue* without doubt conveys, with the help of the blue note as well as by other means for which Gershwin has no one else to thank, a rowdy, troubled humor as marked as that of the best of the old blues. But it is still desirable and, one hopes, possible to keep the term of some value, and one regrets to find in a chapter on the subject by a generally acute observer—a chapter of which half is given over to an interview with Handy—six examples, of which six exhibit no musical characteristic of the blues, old or new, whatever.

But to our blue note. The slur had most commonly accompanied a stressing and perhaps a prolongation of the third by the voice or instrument,—a treatment not possible at every point where that tone might occur, but most characteristic where it coincided with the antepenultimate syllable of a line of the words or appeared as corresponding note in the following "break." And here also, ushering in the cadence, the modern blue note is "in position."

The seventh is similarly treated, though to a less extent, and this secondary blue note has also attracted attention; it is probably responsible for the device (never used by Handy and no doubt native to New Orleans or New York) of ending up the tune on the diminished seventh chord (as Gershwin ended his jazz operetta *135th Street*),—lately sometimes on the chord of the ninth.

The Tangana Rhythm

To Handy also is to be credited the introduction in the accompanying bass of some of his blues, of the Habañera or tango rhythm (a dotted quarter, an eighth and two quarter-notes), which contrasts strikingly

with the syncopation of the air; [25] first used by him in *Memphis Blues* itself. Both the justification for its use in Negro music and the explanation of its subsequent popularity among the Negroes themselves, are supplied on acceptance of the plausible theory [26] that this is an African rhythm (the native word is *tangana*) and Spanish only by adoption through the Moors. Clap your hands, by the way, on the dotted quarter and the eighth-note which follows it in the above example, pat your feet *regularly*, four times to the bar, and you have the Charleston rhythm. Further discussion of the rhythms of the blues would involve survey of a wider subject than can be covered in these remarks, or, competently, by this writer.

The Jazz

The word did not originate in Memphis, and various stories have sprung up to account for it. But with the appearance of the phenomenon itself, the relative shortness of a line of the old blues, as observed and carried into his own writings by Handy, had a tremendous amount to do. That created a gap which human nature could not resist filling in somehow. The singers of the old blues felt obliged, to a "Lawdy," an "Oh, Lawd," an "I said" or "I mean," somehow, to link those two lines together:

Goin' where de Southern cross de Dawg—cross dat Yaller Dawg
Goin' where de Southern cross de Yaller Dawg—cross dat Yaller
  Dawg,—
Goin' where, she cross—dat—Dawg. [27]

It would seldom be more elaborate than these examples, though if he had and played an instrument he might use it to put a little frieze, so to speak, between the capitals, and if he had just heard some one else doing it he might try to do something better if possible or at least different, for here comes in a very powerful racial impulse.

[25] Published in the collection. (ED.)

[26] Friedenthal: *Musik, Tanz und Dichtung bei den Kreolen Amerikas*, page 95, as cited and translated in Krehbiel, and in James Weldon Johnson's preface to The Book of American Negro Spirituals.

[27] And see "Swear to my soul," at page 35,—the interpolated words being as sung by Alberta Hunter in the Paramount record of *Michigan Water Blues;* also "If de river was whisky," at page 40.

That is the impulse of competitive artistic effort,[28]—in singing, of the single voice trying to distinguish itself among the rest, and its strength was noticed by Handy as a child and in the most improbable of circumstances: the singing by large congregations, in the church, of the "baptisin'" and "death-and-burial" songs. These were not spirituals, but old and familiar hymns written in long metre and sung to the old words,—but sung as they never were except by Negroes. Retarded throughout till perhaps ten seconds passed between one syllable and the next, from each note each singer would start off on a little vocal journey of his or her own, wandering up, down or around in strange pentatonic figures, but coming back at the appointed instant to common ground,—the next note of the melody proper. If one had by chance just succeeded in attracting tacit attention by an exceptional note, a striking sequence or rhythmic figure, there would be a dozen others to attempt, starting from the next note, to outdo him, and while the total effect,—chaos to the unaccustomed hearer in the midst of the chorus, but a strange and moving harmony at a distance,—can of course not be transcribed, two examples of how a single voice might run its gamut now follow:

Not this instinct (which should explain the very fact of any variations from air as written at all), but only the common human instinct to fill

[28] For the workings of the impulse in the field of the dance, watch some little colored boys taking turns at the Charleston on the street-corner.

in a gap, was commonly called into action by the folk-blues,—one-man affairs. But with the first performances by a capable Negro orchestra of *Mr. Crump,* something new and unheard-of took place; at a certain point in the third and final air, one musician went wild. He deviated from his score and put in some licks on his own account; he licentiously patted his feet. Up to then this, like every other dance orchestra, had played as best it could what was set before it in black and white; this fellow, indeed, had made himself subject to fine on two counts.[29] But discipline, this time, sat an uneasy saddle, fell, and when encores came, one musician and another would put in his call before the fascinating "break," to fill it, if he could, more ingeniously than his colleagues; to assert his individuality,—just as had his forbears at the baptisin's. The version of the violinist Paul Wyer, already shown at page 48, is the direct descendant of the errant notes of *On Jordan's Stormy Banks.*

The leader had learned something from this; from then on his musicians had carte blanche in the breaks of his blues, of which they, and soon, other Negro bands, made use with gusto. Such things cannot be hid under a bushel, and it was not long before whites were doing the same thing.

Now, the jazz we know, as is obvious but seldom remarked, has two aspects, and it is only as to one that it can be said, all short, in the words of Gilbert Seldes: "1. There is no such thing as jazz music. 2. Jazz is a *method* of playing music." That can be said of one aspect, which is manifested by strange *sounds and tone-qualities,*—raucous squawks, rattles, cowbells, baby-cries, calling for unorthodox instruments, unorthodox treatment of the familiar ones, and tom-toms to mark the beat. Any music can be so played. In the other aspect, however, we find strange *figures;* melodically or rhythmically humorous, angry, passionate or grotesque musical phrases, generally off the main track, subsidiary to the main theme, serving sometimes as an obligato, but most typically as a filler-in of breaks in the melodic mainline. One may say as one way of putting it, that this, too (when improvised), is a method of playing music, but this type of jazz is in the widest sense of the word music in itself, which can be written in ordinary musical notation. The intro-

---

[29] It is interesting to note from his programme that Whiteman cleaves to-day to the same system; his orchestra is "admitted the equal in discipline of any symphony organization." Handy's own theory is that the essence of jazz is spontaneous deviation from the score.

ductory and connecting theme of Rimsky-Korsakoff's *Scheherazade* is not usually referred to as merely a method of playing music, yet when George Gershwin, as Mme. Eva Gauthier's accompanist in the latter's celebrated recital of popular music, inserted at incredible speed that theme between two notes of *Do It Again,* he was beyond question playing jazz. And the soul of Richard Strauss' *Till Eulen-spiegel* goes squealing down to hell to jazz of a very blue tinge. But for the presence of the jazz of strange figures on our every side to-day are responsible Handy, and behind him his band, and behind them, the racial instinct which manifested itself through the congregations of forgotten Negroes in the death and burial songs.

The first aspect of jazz (strange sounds) seized public notice at about the same time as the blues, but its birthplace was probably New Orleans. Whether or not it was called forth by something in the blues need not be argued here, but it was applied to them in that city almost from their first public appearance. Whereas *Memphis Blues* was played in its birthplace with an accompaniment of two slow pats of the foot to the bar (the muffled big drum now supplies this pulse), in New Orleans there would be four quick pats; on the corner of Main and Madison the jazz was confined to the waits, in New Orleans the noise was continuous, threatening to drown out the tune. The prize example of the Louisiana technique, as furnished by the Dixieland Band, is the *Livery Stable Blues,* which was evidently specially built for such usage; the extraordinary if not appalling result has been perpetuated in a Victor record. The New Orleans jazz, as time has worn on, has become far quieter about the house—perhaps it was that or being thrown out altogether—but it remains in its modified condition, and it has had its effect on the tone-quality of the musical type; an effect which is now a part of the general definition. Examples of the musical jazz in the simpler form in which it has generally been written (much simpler than that in which it is often played) were given above by anticipation in the discussion of the folk-blues.[30]

[30] There is a theory that jazz is solely or principally a matter of rhythm,—see a valuable study by Don Knowlton in Harper's Magazine for April, 1926. The writer prefers the view that while perversions and accentuations of rhythm constitute an element of jazz, this feature is subordinate and may be resolved into the two aspects discussed above. The rhythm may be displaced (as by accenting only the recurrent B-flat in the second example at page 42), giving rhythmical jazz of the second type, or it may be marked by the strange sounds of the first.

The success of *Memphis Blues* and its immediate successors resulted very shortly, first in borrowing of the magic word, and then, wholesale, of the jazz idea and of the blue note. Almost every Southern town was endowed (generally from New York) with its private blues, and as the supply of geography dwindled the states came in for the honors; by 1915 they were singing

She cries to him, What's the matter with you?
I've got those Ip-shing, Hong-Kong, Ockaway Chinese *Blues!*

to a tune that still lingers in some memories but would have made Mr. E. H. Crump gasp and stare. Perhaps the first great hit by a white man that showed some real blues about the gills was Cliff Hess' *Homesickness Blues,* of the vintage of 1916. Next year Jim Europe, fresh from the Castle House and equipped with his 15th Infantry Band and Handy's earliest songs, went to France and infected the natives, who commenced writing their ideas of ragtime; at least two Frenchmen (Honegger and Wiener), avowedly their ideas of blues. Even England took enough notice to echo back the name, if little else, in Philip Braham's *Limehouse Blues.* Back in Boston, on a winter night in 1919, prohibition came in while crowds were surging in Washington Street trying to make the rounds from the Parker House to the Holland System before midnight and from behind every swinging door there came the sound of many voices, out-shouting each other in the then heart-breaking words:

I've got the blues, I've got the blues,
I've got the alcoho-olic blues,
No more beer, my heart to cheer,—
Good-bye, Whisky, you used to make me frisky;
So-long Highball! So-long, Gin, Oh,
Tell *me when you're comin', back agin'!*

The blue spirit appealed to Jerome Kern, who copyrighted in 1920 the *Left-All-Alone-Again Blues* (his lyricist, Anne Caldwell, thus starting a fashion of her own of titles of great length denoting the exact nature of the melancholia) and in the following year the *Blue Danube Blues;* to Irving Berlin, of *School-House* and the *Tokio Blues;* John Carpenter, in a frivolous mood, mingled some Katnip and blue notes for the charming *Krazy* and thus qualified as the first "serious" American white composer to flirt with Handy's idea; late in 1925 there was performed by Harry Yerkes' orchestra nothing slighter than a symphony in four movements, *Jazz America,* written by Albert Chiaffarelli and based entirely on the *Beale Street, St. Louis,* and (oddly enough) *Limehouse Blues.* Meanwhile, George Gershwin has made it unanimous among the big three of the musical comedies with (to his brother Ira's lyrics) his *I've Got the You Don't Know the Half of It, Dearie, Blues,* with the *Rhapsody in Blue* and the *Concerto in F.*

Here it is worth while to look back and consider what effect, besides the initial impetus to jazz and the supplanting of the word "rag" as the choice of least resistance for titles, Handy's work has had on American popular music. The latter, for long, has periodically benefited by Afro-American inspirations, which, however, the white borrowers have been able to adapt and carry on with much facility. Thus it was with the white Stephen Foster's work in the lyrical plantation spirit, with the white Ben Harney's (it is claimed to be his) popularization of ragtime in such tunes as the Dummy-Line, stemming from the Gospel Train songs; [31] with the white fashion, started on a long vogue by the remarkable list of successes of the Negroes, Cole and Johnson, derived from the purer spirituals. By this time—about 1906—ragtime was the general idiom, while it was the waltzes and sentimental "ballads" that stuck to the purely white tradition of Dresser and Harris (later, happily, infused, in the case of the waltzes, by Viennese blood); but instrumentally and in particular pianistically, the mode was backward; the air the whole thing, the accompaniment merely strummed. The piano was in line for rescue, however, from its lowly condition, and again it was by a Negro, the gifted and unfortunate Scott Joplin (he fell between the teeth of sharks, lived in wretchedness and died insane) that a new order was ushered in: that of the brilliant and difficult instrumental exercises, the "rags," such as Joplin's own *Maple Leaf,* the prototype of the white Zez Confrey's *Kitten on the Keys.* At this time Jerome D. Kern, who by a hitherto almost unknown harmonic originality and insistence on good writing was powerfully to influence popular music, was devising pleasant little tunes for *The Catch of the Season* and *The Rich Mr. Hoggenheimer,* but he was still nearly ten years from the general applause which

[31] "Jim Crow" songs with syncopated airs, however, were current long before the Civil War, but they lacked the regular beat of ragtime.

began with his *You're Here and I'm Here,* and which still continues. Irving Berlin started later, publishing *Sweet Marie From Sunny Italy* in 1907, and he crashed jubilantly through with *Alexander's Ragtime Band* between the writing and first publication of *Memphis Blues.* When the latter finally burst into the dance halls, it found itself part of a world of popular music which with rare exceptions had one common characteristic—the commonness of which constituted a weakness—it was uniformly one-sided, in a single plane; its colors were all primary. The *Ragtime Band* was all jubilance, the descendants of the coon songs, all animal spirits, the "ballads" (as they are still) all syrup or lugubriousness; the Maple Leaves all sparkle, saying nothing before they finished.

Memphis Blues came with a new and subtler essence, two-sided, and so, disturbing. The campaign enthusiasm and exuberance was there, but there was an undertone of dissent. It suggested, let us say, not only that Mr. Crump was a great fellow, but that if he shouldn't win, things would not be as they should; that things were not right now; perhaps—this in a whisper—that even Mr. Crump couldn't do everything. It was a note, not of weak despondency, but of the divine discontent itself, and this undertone, whether represented by the blue note or any other device, has crept into and enriched, and still enriches, our popular music, transforming it at times from the expression of one of a choice of shallow emotions, to something which can be discussed, under however right or wrong conceptions of what popular music is, as a material fit for building on a larger scale. And it is of the blues spirit and some of the blues devices, be it noted, that Gershwin, the only insistent experimenter along this line whose work is unquestionably worth watching, makes from his own angle a very notable use. Rejecting the tantalizing over-and-over effect of the bob-tailed, twelve-bar strain, which of course would break the long line he would achieve, he has nevertheless made a serious study of the question "wherein blue"; not content with abject imitation, he has thought out the philosophy for himself, making the old tricks somehow his own where he uses them, and making his own point of view the flavor of his work.

But the blue-black is a fast color, and shows no sign of running out. Handy, with the same distaste for mere imitation that distinguishes Gershwin on the other side, has stuck to his native language and thus not only kept the piquancy of his work for the alien, but secured its joyful acceptance by his own race—something the white man's impressions of the musical Negro had failed to do,—for his starting in, after forty years as one of and with them, to write as they sang and talked, resulted in something genuine. If he improved upon a crude wail that none but himself would have noticed, he improved it in its original direction, as would have any Southern Negro with natural talent, in singing it for the amusement of those about him. If, instead, he drew on his notable fund of melody, it was in the same vein. So his people would take his tunes to their bosoms and promptly commence making new verses for them, or adapting old ones. So much of this has been done since he began writing that it would be impossible without exhaustive research to place this or that verse quoted in this very book as pre- or post-Handy; some may be heard on the "race-records" to tunes sung by Ma Rainey and her competitors; they have been used, in each case, after an investigation indicating that they were not written for the occasion, but repeated—but some may have been written for other occasions. Folk song is not, however, dead even in this day and land, and it is not even exclusively negroid, and the succinct form of the blues has something that calls for new ideas to fit it. The average is not compact of wit and imagination as it is written, but it assays as a whole far higher than the type turned out by the white lyricists. Most of the latter would afford a painful comparison with Handy's own verses: with the bizarre flavor of

> (*I've put some*)
> ASHES *in my sweet papa's bed,*
> *So that he can't slip out—*
> HOODOO, *in his bread,*
> *Goopher-dust all about—*I'll fix him!—
> CON-JU-RA-TION
> *Is in his socks and shoes;*
> *To-morrow, he will have those*
> *Mean Sundown Blues!*

his satire on the prissy and citified Harlemite:

> *The man I love's got low-down ways for sure,*
> *The man I love's got low-down ways for sure,*
> *Well, I am hinkty,*[32] *and I'm low-down too.*

[32] "Hinkty"—the old-time darkey—"handkerchief-head." Cf. "blanket Indian."

He *don't gay-cattin' 'roun' with dicty* [33] *cats.*
Don't go gay-cattin' roun' in buffet flats,—
We like our basement, an' our basement rats!

You can keep your attics, take the roof or the air if you choose,
You can keep your attics, take the roof or the air if you choose,
But my *highest aspiration is the Basement Blues.*

(patter:)

High-falutin' lowbrows under gobs of paint,
Pretendin' like they is, when they know darn well they ain't.
Lots of high-brow low-brows, I'm tellin' you a fac',
Too many pop-eyed pots a-callin' bow-legged kittles black.

Beale Street of the old days summed up in one line:

You'll fin' dat business never closes, till somebody gets killed.

Yellow Dog—a long, long, story on a postcard:

Dear Sue: *Your Easy Rider struck this burg to-day,*
On a south-boun' rattler, side-door Pullman car;
Seen him here, an he was on the hog.[34]
The smoke was broke, no joke,—not a jitney on him.

Easy Rider's got to stay away, so he
Had to vamp it,[35] *but the hike ain't far,—*
He's gone where the Southern cross the Yellow Dog.[36]

Both races have contributed to the ascendancy of the real blues, and in the beginning, in the face of much prejudice. The first mention should be of the original Handy's Band of *Mr. Crump,* of which the first-string men were Ed and Paul Wyer and Jim Turner, violins; Archie Walls, bass viol; George Higgins, guitar and vocalist; George Williams, trombone; Robert Young, clarinet; James Osborne, saxophone (and one of the first in any orchestra; he got religion and went to the House of David); Handy himself played the cornet.

[33] "Dicty"—uppish and conceited.
[34] "On the hog"—broke.
[35] "Vamp it"—make it on his vamps—walk it.
[36] "Yellow Dog"—the Yazoo Delta Railroad, which crosses the Southern at Morehead, Mississippi.

Other bands must not be forgotten: Handy's second string, through which the Columbia Company put Tennessee into every other state; Eddie Cupero's band of the Honey-Boy Evans Minstrels, bravely pictured on the cover of the vocal edition of *Memphis Blues;* Wilbur C. Sweatman's, which carried to the country through Pathé and Emerson records the echo of old Joe Turney and his chain-gangs.

Of a mighty line of contraltos, the deep voice of Ma Rainey, of the necklace of gold eagles, was perhaps the first upraised before the public; it is still heard in the land, directly and through race records of the Paramount Company, but to-day the Smiths alone of her competitors number no less than five, all colored: the vivacious Clara, billed as The World's Greatest Moaner; mournful Trixie; Laura, a charter member of the guild; Mamie, the first of her race and sex to record a typical negroid popular song (it was Perry Bradford's *You Can't Keep a Good Man Down*); and Bessie, The Empress, who makes up her own words before the unforgiving jaws of the recording machine. A white Smith, Joe, featured in *Yellow Dog Blues* for the Victor, for the first time on any record, the demoniac laugh of an instrument (in this case trombone) played by Harry Raderman, the originator. Raderman carried the laugh to Ted Lewis' Band, where it spread to the saxophones; any one who heard that redoubtable organization playing the Handy blues, or the war-time *Smiles,* will hardly have forgotten it. But back to the singers: Alice Leslie Carter, colored, who in a rathskeller under the Columbia Burlesque Theater, introduced *Memphis Blues* (as a song) to Broadway; Alberta Hunter, a well-known voice on the records, who introduced *Loveless Love* at the Dreamland cabaret in Chicago; the inimitable String Beans, who to an accompaniment of hisses from out front would improvise verses to his own blues tunes throughout his turn at the old Monogram Theater (a standby of Chicago Negroes); his audience loved, but felt they should hate him, so they would pack the place night after night, swearing they came to see the acrobats and would never return while String Beans remained—but staying always, rooted to their seats, till his little personal *Home, Sweet Home*:

> *If any one asks you, has String Beans been along,*
> *If any one asks you, has String Beans been along,—*
> *Jus' tell 'em String Beans been here, done got his, an' gone.*

Perhaps no one has transcribed more blues as sung by illiterate Negroes than Dave Peyton (former orchestra leader at the Grand Theater, Chicago, and now musical editor of the Chicago Defender) and Lovie Austin,[37] who used to arrange String Beans' tunes for the Monogram orchestra, and now performs a similar function in the making of racial records for the Paramount Company. The Leighton Brothers, white men, who by their arrangement and publication, with a rousing chorus, of *Frankie and Johnny* started large sections of the nation digging up the old verses, early recognized the uses of the blues, though white singers were not so quick to take them up. Blossom Seeley, however, sang *Hesitating Blues* in 1916; Marie Cahill's name is written large in cerulean letters; Gilda Gray and Beale Street helped make each other famous; Marion Harris has the manner so at her command that thousands of Negroes make a point of buying her records, under the impression that she is one of them. Of students, few have noticed the place of the blues in folksong, while as popular music, of course, they fall under a general condemnation. But the Negro, James Weldon Johnson,[38] was perhaps the first writer to call attention to the roots which Handy had uncovered; Miss Dorothy Scarborough, undervaluing the fundamental importance of the form in the blues definition, nevertheless has not failed to realize that the type was, up to a definite point, one of natural and unconscious growth; Carl Van Vechten has loved the blues, and on frequent occasions and in no uncertain terms has admitted and justified the fact.[39] The songs, and the notes thereto, in this collection, will speak for the Negro composers in the old tradition, with the exception of Clarence Williams; not represented, but deserving of mention here for his work on paper, on the records, and before the footlights.

[37] Daughter of Arthur Calhoun. Professor Calhoun was Roland Hayes' first singing teacher and is now organist of the one church in New York where the spirituals, the shouts and the Gospel Train songs may be heard to-day as in the old South.

[38] Before wide recognition of his poetical and other abilities, a member of the famous song-writing team which comprised also his brother Rosamond and Bob Cole; they sometimes wrote, strange to say, under the pen-name of "Will Handy."

[39] See in particular his articles in *Vanity Fair* for August, 1925, and March, 1926, the former of which contains some verses not included herein and numerous facts which are.

Notes on Boogie-Woogie

WILLIAM RUSSELL
from *HRS Rag*

William Russell, known to his friends as the Lama of Jazz, is one of the most painstaking of critics. He has written little, in comparison to his reputation, but what he has written made its mark. As one of the writers of the epoch-making Jazzmen, *he can claim a unique position in the annals of jazz criticism. During the life of the* HRS Rag, *an alternately scholarly and irreverent jazz magazine which had on its staff Charles Edward Smith and Steve Smith, Bill Russell wrote some of the most penetrating reviews of jazz ever to appear in any magazine—and that includes* Jazz Information. *Two of these reviews, dealing with important boogie-woogie issues by Dan Qualey's Solo Art and by Blue Note, are joined together here because they deserve permanence between the covers of a book. Russell has quit critical writing and devotes himself to the record field—the American Music label is his—but he can have no objection to seeing these words of his in print again. (ED.)*

THE Blue Note Meade "Lux" Lewis piano solos[1] again bring to the limelight the talents of this highly imaginative artist. His brilliant 12-inch recording of *Honky Tonk Train Blues* recalls to mind the greatness and vitality of a phenomenal composition which must be regarded as a masterpiece of modern music.

That two seasons of countless repetition of the *Honky Tonk*, in a necessarily stereotyped two minute version, failed to curb Lux's imagination or his enthusiasm is amply proven by his latest recording session.

The *Honky Tonk* is taken at an amazing speed. Although the piece

[1] Blue Note 15 and 16.

is almost impossible for an ordinary pianist to attempt, even at a more moderate tempo, and misleads many trained listeners into believing that it is for two pianists, the music is so pianistic that the notes actually fall right under the fingers. It is interesting to observe that although the composition is in the key of G, the left hand is so arranged as to use only the white keys.

Fig. 1

Of further interest is the unconventional use of "four-six" chords throughout. The fact that the tonic chord does not really appear until the final note of the piece may account partly for the suspense as well as the feeling of momentum which Meade Lux produces.

The characteristic rhythmic devices which Lux uses, such as the cross rhythms of the second and third chorus, are perhaps even more exciting at the rapid tempo used on the Blue Note recording.

Fig. 2

Meade "Lux" Lewis has always been a marvel of inexhaustible inventiveness, and the new *Honky Tonk* contains eight effective and highly stimulative variations heretofore unrecorded in the shorter versions. The new *Honky Tonk* comes to a close with the familiar final variation:

Fig. 3

which further illustrates the ability of Lux to create great swing and rhythmic effect from apparently so simple a polymetrical device.

Tell Your Story is a moderately fast boogie woogie blues. The left hand plays a bass figure of even 8ths with insistent drumlike pounding. The bass, as well as certain melodic features, resemble the style often used by Pete Johnson. More remarkable than this evidence of Lux's long association with Pete at Cafe Society is his skill and discriminating taste in the selection of ideas and in formulating his distinctive and unmistakable style. Just as Lux once assimilated the best elements of the Yancey blues style and the Cripple Clarence stomp style (*Tell Your Story*—9th and 10th choruses) he has now adapted ideas from Pete Johnson into his—the most personal of all boogie woogie styles. Everything he plays bears his indisputable trademark. In his feeling for the subtleties of piano resonance, the sensitivity to tone color, the independence of hands in rhythmic complexities, as well as in the mastery of form by means of unity, compositional organization, and climactic development, Meade Lux has probably not been equalled by any known boogie woogie pianist.

Another striking feature of Lewis' talent is his ability to make the piano seem a part of his being in expressing his feelings. Not only is the piano intrinsically a colder, less direct, and more mechanical means of individual expression than many instruments, but it also lacks the means of sounding the microtones (such as the lowered 3rd and 7th) and sliding tones peculiar to the scalar and harmonic structure which has long been regarded as essential to the blues style. Somehow Lux bridges the gap and makes the piano as intimately personal and expressive an instrument as a singer's vocal chords.

In producing a feeling of blues harmony and off-scale colors, he rarely resorts to the use of minor and diminished chords, but rather creates his impressions through the use of dissonance. Frequently his chords are built of clusters of superimposed seconds. Not that Lux makes an intellectual application of the theory of dissonant chord structure, but apparently he has the inherent faculty of "feeling out" the most poignant and appropriate tone colors for the blues.

As a master of rhythmic subtleties, Lux is also unsurpassed. The unaccompanied introduction of *Bass On Top* consists of a series of single notes, not one of which is played exactly on the metrical pulse, yet the tempo is instantly indicated and a rocking swing immediately set up as Lux's pudgy fingers pound out the staggering rhythm. Just as in the *Honky Tonk Train,* Lux again proves that the most striking and effective music can be produced by the most natural and simple means.

Bass On Top is a remarkable composition in which a rhythmic and a melodic germ motive are developed over a "walking bass" figure.

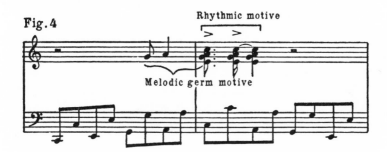

The rhythmic motive, consisting of two sharply accented chords, is augmented to form the *Charleston* rhythm (variations 2 to 4); is elaborated by extension (variations 6 and 7); is reversed in variation 8. This rhythm which might be considered as the retrograde form of the *Charleston* rhythm has always been a predominant rhythm in the boogie woogie. In variation 9, two forms of the rhythmic motive are combined.

A still more ingenious development is made of the 3 note melodic motive. Lewis' music has occasionally been compared to that of Bach in its grandeur and sweep, and in its usage of improvisational and contrapuntal technique. However in *Bass On Top* the motival development is more suggestive of Beethoven's painstaking elaboration. Naturally Lux did not consciously set out to develop his motives as systematically and laboriously as did Beethoven in his sketch books, but nevertheless, a masterful use of his material is made. The germ motive itself is derived from the bass accompaniment figure. It is treated by extension (chorus 2) by diminution and inversion (choruses 4 and 6) twisted and turned about until its possibilities of elaboration are seemingly exhausted. Finally, in the eleventh chorus there begins a liquidation in which not only the melodic but the rhythmic motive and accompanying bass figure, as well, are reduced to their most essential features.

Six Wheel Chaser is another breathtaking piece of tremendous drive and elemental power. The bass resembles the figure used in *Honky Tonk Train Blues,* except that the chords are in root position. The music, often consisting only of repeated notes, chords, or short motives, has little melodic tunefulness. Pulsating percussive chords, such as Meade Lux uses in the sixth chorus, produce a powerful syncopated momentum. What Stravinsky probably felt and tried to do in parts of *Le Sacre,* Lux accomplishes with a minimum of tonal, technical, and instrumental resources.

Throughout the record there is an impelling logic to his rhythmic development. As his ideas unfold with incredible drive, and at times with frenetic outbursts of crushing force, the rhythm is not the only factor of interest. Fascinating and amazing sonorities occur during the surging of tone.

Boogie woogie, though cast in the structural and harmonic form of the blues, often (as in the case of *Six Wheel Chaser*) has little of blues *feeling,* but is more a jubilant stomp-like dance of rugged energy.

Small wonder that Lux's chubby hands were tired after three hours of pounding out the terrific music he recorded on that September night for Blue Note.

Among Solo Art's releases are solos by four outstanding boogie-woogie pianists—Pete Johnson, Albert Ammons, Meade Lux Lewis, and Cripple Clarence Lofton. In keeping with his fantastic and enigmatic career, Clarence again does the unbelievable and, even among this fast company, carries off honors as the month's most exciting soloist.

Cripple Clarence could well be regarded as the personification of crude, illiterate musicianship. And by the same token Clarence might be hailed as the ultimate in vitality, freshness, and originality.

It is a generally accepted fact that refinement and elaboration in any art are accompanied by a corresponding decline in vital ruggedness, spirited abandon, and in genuineness and intensity in power of expression. If one had any doubt of the validity of this observation in application to hot jazz, one need only consider the spontaneity, breadth, and forceful expressiveness of the early and cruder Hot Five records. Although Louis had technique to spare he played like a veritable wildman on his early records; and as for Ory and Dodds—they always sounded as though their instruments were in danger of being blown to bits.

Cripple Clarence would appear to be good evidence in support of the theory that the origin of boogie-woogie was due to lack of pianistic skill among those self-taught musicians who were compelled to keep their left hand in one position and constantly repeat a figure.

Clarence takes *Pinetop's Boogie Woogie* and virtually murders it. Some of the rough outlines are crudely sketched with broad strokes and there is no difficulty during the first part in recognizing what Lofton is trying to play, but soon he rambles off, guided only by his own most individual and productive imagination. Clarence, who boasts that Pine Top was "his boy," and who attempts to show Yancey and Lux how to play, would not hesitate to cut Rachmaninoff, were he by mistake to get into Chicago's Orchestra Hall some evening.

In recent years there has appeared a lot of pretentious nonsense about the unconventional length of the "conventional 12 bar blues." Those who rave about this unusual "folk pattern" would have a tough time explaining Clarence's peculiar phrase and period lengths. In his version of *Pine Top's Boogie Woogie,* his first three choruses are respectively—eleven, ten, and twelve measures in length. In the latter part of the piece Clarence favors a fourteen bar construction, with a final chorus of fourteen and a half for good measure. Odd phrase lengths were likewise in his previous Solo Art recording of *Streamline Train—Had a Dream,* and in *I Don't Know,* in which pairs of nineteen and twenty bar

choruses are followed by one of nineteen and a half. Quite evidently
Clarence did not set out either to make his music screwy, or mathe-
matically complicated—he just plays the notes to express what he feels,
and can't be bothered to count out the number of beats. After all,
Clarence does not even regard himself as a pianist, but simply as a
singing entertainer who has made good money in his day. "Man, Ah've
made as much as $3.00 a night."

Actually, according to Mr. Petrillo (who incidentally admits he can't
tell any difference between Heifetz and a tavern fiddler) Clarence is
just an amateur. Once upon a time Clarence was accustomed to rove
around the vast desolate spaces of the dilapidated and dark South State
Street section, stopping in every joint that had a piano, "breaking it
down" as soon as the regular pianist or orchestra got off the stand, But
never having collected enough cash to join the union, he has been
chased out of all the dives in which he was once welcome.

An amateur is not to be regarded however with condescension. A
perusal of the history of music and other arts shows that many important creative innovations have been due to the amateur. Usually in art
a new style has its inceptions with the people, and not with cultivated
performers. Although Clarence has his own kind of virtuosity which
could never be matched by any professional concert pianist, he has
preserved much of the freshness, originality, and especially the enthusiasm of an amateur. He has the rare quality of being able to *send*
himself, and is not dependent upon the inspiration of others, or certain
favorable conditions, for a rousing performance.

Absolute steadiness in tempo is often considered one of the most
essential skills of a good musician. An examination of Clarence's tempi
discloses that not only is his closing tempo usually faster than the beginning, but that certain phrases within this gradual acceleration are
frequently rushed or retarded. Unless one believes that metronomic
rigidity is the rule of life, one must admit that Lofton's free and perhaps
even lax procedure is more natural and normal. Certainly the effective-
ness and excitement of many dances call for constantly accelerated tempi.
It is rather an arbitrary and illogical standard which requires an im-
mobile tempo to be maintained, as though the body of the dancer, once
set in motion, must be considered a mechanical clock piece.

Just as Clarence plays in only two different keys, "C" and "G," he tends to maintain his tempi, in all his pieces, around two general speed centers —fast (about 126) and slow (92).

I Don't Know is one of the most amazing piano solos ever waxed. After an amusing one-finger introduction (even then he hits a bum note), Clarence drives into his prize piece with great zest. This solo was originally a vocal number and after five choruses, in place of a vocal, there occurs a most unusual interlude which sounds somewhat like the "vamp till ready" introductions of early ragtime days.

Especially in the left hand part, with its frequent open fifths in the manner of medieval organum, a distinct modal feeling is prevalent. Actually the bass line does lie within the Dorian mode. As Clarence develops the queer interlude motif and combines it with the original thematic material, some very weird and interesting clashing of harmonies occurs. Accidentally or otherwise, Clarence has stumbled across the most unusual harmony ever used in a blues or boogie woogie composition. No one can complain of "monotonous tonic and dominant" harmonies in *I Don't Know*.

When Qualey hopped the bus and went to Chicago to record Clarence, he pulled a real prize out of the bag. Maybe Clarence never in his life got a vote in a favorite musicians poll, but there are more kicks and original ideas per inch on these sides than the big ten ever put on record.

Jazz in America

JEAN-PAUL SARTRE
from *Les Cahiers America*

During a visit to New York in the mid-Forties, Jean-Paul Sartre, the French philosopher, visited Nick's in Greenwich Village. He not only listened to the wide-open Dixieland jazz for which the place is noted; he also observed the people there. His ironic article is not music criticism but existentialist commentary—doubly interesting because the French as a rule approach jazz with an intense, almost naïve, serious-ness. Sartre's vignette was first published in a special jazz issue of Les Cahiers America. *It was subsequently published, in my translation, by* The Saturday Review of Literature. (ED.)

Jazz is like bananas—it must be consumed on the spot. God knows there are recordings in France, and some sad imitators. But all they do is give us an excuse to shed a few tears in pleasant company. Like everyone else, I really discovered jazz in America. Some coun-tries have a national pastime and some do not. It's a national pastime when the audience insists on complete silence during the first half of the performance and then shouts and stamps during the second half. If you accept this definition, France has no national pastime, unless it is auction sales. Nor has Italy, except stealing. There is watch-ful silence while the thief works (first half) and when he flees there is stamping and shouts of "Stop, thief" (second half). Belgium has its cockfights, Germany vampirism, and Spain its *corridas*.

I learned in New York that jazz is a national pastime. In Paris, it is a vehicle for dancing, but this is a mistake: American don't dance to jazz; instead they have a special music, heard also at marriages and First Communions, called: Music by Muzak. In apartments there is a faucet. It is turned on and Muzak musics: flirtation, tears, dancing. The faucet is turned off, and Muzak musics no more: the lovers and communicants are put to bed.

At Nick's bar, in New York, the national pastime is presented. Which means that one sits in a smoke-filled room among sailors, Orientals, chippies, society women. Tables, booths. No one speaks. The sailors come in fours. With justified hatred, they watch the smoothies who sit in booths with their girls. The sailors would like to have the girls, but they don't. They drink; they are tough; the girls are also tough; they drink, they say nothing. No one speaks, no one moves, the jazz holds forth. From ten o'clock to three in the morning the jazz holds forth. In France, jazzmen are beautiful but stupid, in flowing shirts and silk ties. If you are too bored to listen, you can always watch them and learn about elegance.

At Nick's bar, it is advisable not to look at them; they are as ugly as the musicians in a symphony orchestra. Bony faces, mustaches, business suits, starched collars (at least in the early part of the evening), no velvety looks, muscles bunching up under their sleeves.

They play. You listen. No one dreams. Chopin makes you dream, but not the jazz at Nick's. It fascinates, you can't get your mind off it. No consolation whatsoever. If you are a cuckold, you depart a cuckold, with no tenderness. No way to take the hand of the girl beside you, to make her understand, with a wink, that the music reflects what is in your heart. It is dry, violent, pitiless. Not gay, not sad, inhuman. The cruel screech of a bird of prey. The musicians start to give out, one after the other. First the trumpet player, then the pianist, then the trombonist. The bass player grinds it out. It does not speak of love, it does not comfort. It is hurried. Like the people who take the subway or eat at the Automat.

It is not the century-old chant of Negro slaves. Nor the sad little dream of Yankees crushed by the machine. Nothing of the sort: there is a fat man who blows his lungs out to the weaving motion of his trumpet, there is a merciless pianist, a bass player who tortures the strings without listening to the others. They are speaking to the best part of you, the toughest, the freest, to the part which wants neither melody nor refrain, but the deafening climax of the moment. They take hold of you, they do not lull you. Connecting rod, shaft, spinning top. They beat you, they turn, they crash, the rhythm grips you and shakes you. You bounce in your seat, faster and faster, and your girl with you, in a hellish round.

The trombone sweats, you sweat, the trumpet sweats, you sweat some more, and then you feel that something has happened on the bandstand; the musicians don't look the same: they speed ahead, they infect each other with this haste, they look mad, taut, as if they were searching for something. Something like sexual pleasure. And you too begin to look for something. You begin to shout; you have to shout; the band has become an immense spinning top: if you stop, the top stops and falls over. You shout, they shriek, they whistle, they are possessed, you are possessed, you scream like a woman in child-birth. The trumpet player touches the pianist and transmits his hypnotic obsession. You go on shouting. The whole crowd shouts in time, you can't even hear the jazz, you watch some men on a bandstand sweat-ing in time, you'd like to spin around, to howl at death, to slap the face of the girl next to you.

And then, suddenly, the jazz stops, the bull has received the sword thrust, the oldest of the fighting cocks is dead. It's all over. But you have drunk your whisky, while shouting, without even knowing it. An impassive waiter has brought you another. For a moment, you are in a stupor, you shake yourself, you say to your girl: Not bad. She doesn't answer, and it begins all over again. You will not make love tonight, you will not feel sorry for yourself, you will not even be sur-feited, you won't get real drunk, you won't even shed blood, and you'll have undergone a fit of sterile frenzy. You will leave a little worn out, a little drunk, but with a kind of dejected calm, the aftermath of nervous exhaustion.

Jazz is the national pastime of the United States.

They Sang in Jazz

RALPH de TOLEDANO
from *National Review*

I. Bessie Smith

To THE world of jazz, and to the Negro audiences which packed the vaudeville houses where she sang, she was just Bessie Smith—the greatest blues singer to come out of the South. Bessie Smith was a big woman—two hundred and ten pounds of energy and muscle and temperament. When she was born will never be known and how she died, on a September night in 1937, has already become part of a mythology. Her roots were in Chattanooga, and it was not far from there that she was killed in an automobile crash which tore off an arm. She might have been saved, the story goes, had not a white hospital refused to admit her before she bled to death.

If this account is true, then she was one more victim on the altar of man's inhumanity. But in a sense, she was already dead before her heart stopped beating. Liquor had already driven away the booking agents—and the Negro public which once bought her records by the millions had turned to other music and other gods. In her day, she had earned $1,500 a week almost every week, but wild extravagance and wilder living squandered it all. Perhaps she might have made a comeback in the swingtime of the 1930's, but this is doubtful. For Bessie Smith belonged to a golden era when the music was rich and unrefined, and the ear of jazz still sensitive to folk nuance.

We some of us saw Bessie last in 1936, at a Sunday jam session in the dark shadows of the old Famous Door on 52nd Street. But the years of failure, of singing in cheap nightclubs and dives, had left their mark on her and she blinked in bewilderment at the "serious" jazz students who regarded her as a museum piece. The idea of becoming the object of sociological inquiry bored Bessie. She loved the glitter of success—but barring this Bessie preferred the gin and noise and earthy attention of the musical backstreets which still claimed her.

Yet nothing could erase from that hewn mahogany face the days of her glory. Sheathed in white satin and caught in the embrace of the big spot, she had given the splendid or vulgar songs of her people a passion beyond their simple content. In the recording studios, she had engraved them on one hundred and sixty pieces of wax, surrounded by the best jazz musicians of the time—lifting them up to the mournful or brash fervor of her singing and being lifted up by them in turn. Tender or raucous, instrumental voice and vocal instrument had blended into an expression as deep as the Sorrow Songs which we call spirituals. Untutored she was—and violent in her gin—but she knew her worth and would not have it pawed by college boys.

"Ma" Rainey, a blues singer closer to the taproots of the blues, found Bessie. "Ma" heard the raw teenager sing and realized with sure intuition that here was something unique. Bessie could be taught phrasing and intonation, the notes to hold and those to throw away, when to ride with a tune and when to subvert it to her own purpose. But the voice was there, with all its overtones of pain and exaltation— a voice which could shake a theatre in the days before microphones. The genius which reaches across the footlights, which transmutes the inert mass of an audience into a living participant, was intuitive. In 1923, Frank Walker of Columbia records heard Bessie singing in an Alabama honky-tonk, recorded her, and made history. Her first record outsold everything in the catalogue.

All that remains today is the nostalgia and the records—the best of them gathered together on four Columbia LPs by George Avakian. It is an amazing and priceless legacy: Bessie and Louis Armstrong adding a new dimension to *St. Louis Blues,* the warm-timbred cornet in counterpoint or filling in the breaks; Bessie and James P. Johnson, the intricate suspended rhythms of his piano making a duet of *Backwater Blues;* Bessie and Joe Smith, the quiet purity of his now-forgotten cornet in moving commentary to her harsher threnody in *Weeping Willow Blues;* Bessie on her last recording date, rowdy and abrasive in a merciless evocation of Harlem rent parties, the everyday death of loveless love, the unquenchable spirit of a singer who knew she had fallen off the golden bandstand.

The artistry goes beyond this. For Bessie could take a tune as uninspired as *Alexander's Ragtime Band* or as vacuously suggestive as

Empty Bed Blues and give them pertinency. There was no one like her before, and there has been no one like her since. Wherever she sang, she cried out her defiance of the human condition and accepted its tragedy. When she died, something of music died with her—and something of life.

II. Billie Holiday

I REMEMBER Billie Holiday singing *Strange Fruit* around the eddying cigarette smoke of Café Society Downtown. It was a Popular Front song about lynching ("Strange fruit hanging from the poplar trees") sung for a Popular Front audience in a Greenwich Village nightclub. But it had its power and its validity in the exquisite torture of her voice, in the ungainly beauty of a dark face flatly delineated by the baby spots.

Those were great days for Billie Holiday, when jazz was the real and the true, when she was recording against the background of Teddy Wilson's delicately contrived rhythm, the outburst of Artie Shaw's clarinet, and the limpid alto saxophone of Johnny Hodges, or the clear, sweet tone of Bunny Berigan's cornet. Those were the days of *Billie's Blues,* out of the deep South via Harlem, of *Summertime,* in pounding accents that would have startled George Gershwin, of two wonderfully evocative tunes, *Easy Living* and *Foolin' Myself.* This was Billie before the demons moved in.

Then the rich boys and social consciousness took over, and so did the marijuana and the drugs. Billie continued to sing, but she had a monkey on her back—and the corruption of courts and hospitals and the "cure" which never really cured. Now Billie is dead, and those of us who knew her—however fleetingly—can mourn. But she left her music for others who now put record to turntable. Any song, good or banal, acquired new stature when she sang it. Her phrasing was impeccable, and her sense of the *rubato*—that straying behind and around the beat which characterizes jazz singing—was perfect. She would wander from the melody until the split second which the trained ear knows, and then return with a glorious resolution. Toward the end of her life, what had been a plangently full voice developed an astringency, a spareness, but she never lost the complete mastery of the phrase, the knowledge of a song's inner logic.

These are superlatives—but they apply to a singer superlatively confounded by success or failure or sex or the tragedy of drug addiction, but always singing as her artistry dictated. Her Verve album, *Solitude,* is a case in point. From Cole Porter's adolescently ironic *Love for Sale* to the Triangle Club's whimsical *East of the Sun,* Billie took over these songs and gave them to jazz. The Porter lyrics can be mawkish in their traversal of vice as seen by the romantic undergraduate; but Billie made them poignant and meaningful as vice can be when it ceases to be posturing. *Easy to Love* and *Everything I Have Is Yours,* which in the 1930's we hummed on forgotten dance floors, became jazz *lieder* when they were transfigured by Billie's bitter-sweet interpretation.

It was Billie Holiday's special talent to invigorate and illuminate the product that Tin Pan Alley threw into the music market. The slightly mocking overtones of her singing, paradoxically, did not result in parody but in a heightening of meaning. She could move into an oldie like *Just One More Chance,* which Russ Colombo mooed into prominence, and give it the urgency of unrequited love. *Baby Won't You Please Come Home,* pounded into a razz-ma-tazz of oompah by innumerable Dixieland bands, she returned to a meaningful jazz context. Even *You Took Advantage of Me,* a specialty of Bing Crosby in his soprano days with the Rhythm Boys, surrendered to the Holiday attack.

Year after year, in sickness and in health, Billie's recorded output continued. (The best of her early records were gathered together in a Columbia LP, *Lady Day.*) Sometimes, during the bad years, only the manner remained. But this was often enough. With Billie gone, what Negro singer can take her place? Ella Fitzgerald has her great moments. But she has never been of Billie's complex musical persuasion—nor does she draw so deeply from the well of jazz.

You return inevitably to Billie—the Billie Holiday we applauded in smoky rooms, the Billie Holiday in shimmering satin who stood before the bands of the 1930's in the vast caverns of now-vanishing movie palaces, the Billie Holiday who all her life could sing and mean, "If you let me love you, it's for sure I'll love you all the way."

King Oliver

PRESTON JACKSON
from *Hot News*

Preston Jackson, who played in the famous series of dates which at-
tempted a re-creation of New Orleans Jazz for Decca, is an old-timer
from the Crescent City. Students of Delaunay's discography can trace
his history and listen to the records he made with some of the New
Orleans titans. In the Thirties, he did a lot of writing for the British and
French hot jazz publications. These reminiscences of King Oliver ap-
peared in the now-defunct Hot News *and are, in a sense, a sort of*
documentary. (ED.)

I DON'T know who was the first man to play modern style trumpet, but
the earliest exponent who is still playing [1] must be Joe, or as you call
him, "King," Oliver. Joe is a native of New Orleans, my own home town,
and I have known him since 1912. I was very young then, but Joe was
much older, and had been playing trumpet for a number of years.

Though he was near the top in the early days of jazz, he had a lot of
competition, for there were plenty of good trumpet players then, just
as there are nowadays. Willie Hightower, Mutt Carey, Tig Chambers,
Freddie "King" Keppard, Celestin, Manuel Poree,[2] and a lot of others
were all fine players, though I doubt if you ever heard of any of these
fellows. Some of them never recorded and never will. Some of them are
dead; poor Freddie Keppard drank himself to death.

Mutt Carey was a particularly fine player: Muggsy reminds me of
him a lot. Mutt never could play high, but he made Joe Oliver throw
his trumpet away once. There was a big parade in New Orleans and
Mutt was with the Tuxedo Brass Band, while Joe was with the Onward

1 When this was written, Oliver was still alive—a tragic, broken man trying to make a
comeback with a "swing" band, but too poor and unknown to push into the graces of a
forgetful public. (ED.)
2 Perez? (ED.)

Brass Band. His outfit was a few feet in front of the Tuxedo band in the parade and Mutt was playing some grand stuff. Joe couldn't take it long. He just threw his horn away and went into a pawnshop and bought another.

Later on, about 1914 I should say, Joe began to improve a lot. He used to practice very hard. I remember he once told me that it took him ten years to get a tone on his instrument. He used a half-cocked mute, and how he could make it talk! He played the variation style too; running chords I mean. His ear was wonderful—that helped a lot.

One of the best numbers I ever heard Joe play was *Eccentric*. He took all the breaks, imitating a rooster, and a baby. He was a riot, in those days, his band from 1915 or 16 to 1918 being the best in New Orleans. The La Rocca boys of the Dixieland Jazz Band used to hang around and got a lot of ideas from his gang. The boys playing with Joe then were Johnny Dodds, clarinet; Edward Ory, trombone; Ed. Garland, bass viol; Henry Zeno, drums; Eddie Polla, violin; and a guitar player whose name I have forgotten. He didn't use a piano. How those boys could swing, and it was jazz they played, too, not ragtime music.

Louis Armstrong was coming along strong about this time. He was just beginning to make people sit up and take notice.

The first jazz band, the New Orleans Jazz Band, was in Chicago at about this time, having come North a year or two before. It was a sensation in Chicago, New York, and everywhere it played. Bill Johnson, bass viol, used to lead, and he had Freddie Keppard on trumpet, with George Bakay,[3] clarinet; Ed. Vincent, trombone; Cottrell, drums; and Ed. Polla, violin and sax.

Then Sidney Bechet came to Chicago. (He went to England later.) He was the King. He couldn't read a note, but could play anything. It is said that the first time he picked up a clarinet he played like a veteran. Sid is with Noble Sissle now. He, Johnny Dodds, and Teo, were rivals, and three of the greatest clarinetists ever known. Teo schooled both Barney Bigard and Albert Nicholas.

When Joe Oliver came to Chicago in 1918 he was regarded as the King of the trumpet. He played at the Dreamland Cafe from 8 till 1.00 A.M., and would then go to the Pekin Cafe and play until 6.00 A.M.

[3] Bacquet. (ED.)

His made the second big band in Chicago—and both came from New Orleans.

The next to come was Tig Chambers and his band. Tig was marvellous, and so was his trombone player, Roy Palmer. With these three bands Chicago musicians didn't have a chance.

There were a lot of keen youngsters around in those days. Buster Bailey was a kid just beginning, while Tommy Ladnier was only just starting out. I didn't play anything then, but was thinking of taking the clarinet. I used to sit on the bandstand all night, listening.

After a while Joe Oliver went to the Lincoln Gardens, and that is where he really hit his stride. The New Orleans Rhythm Kings were there every night too. It was common to see musicians writing on their cuffs in those days. Rapollo, the Rhythm Kings' clarinetist, was always writing—and his numbers are still played today. Jelly Roll Morton was around, too. He was considered the best piano player; Earl Hines was unheard of.

Joe still had the same band, but he finally got a pianist, a lady named Lottie Taylor. After that he had Lil Hardin, who later became Mrs. Louis Armstrong. Then Joe sent for Louis to join him as second trumpet.

Oh Boy! Did those two team together? When you saw Joe lean over towards Louis at the first ending you would know they were going to make a break in the middle of the next chorus. And what breaks they made. Louis never knew what Joe was going to play, but he would always follow him perfectly. Louis was, and is, as good a second trumpet as he is a first; he never missed. They played together for three or four years and wrote some numbers together. One of them was *Dipper-Mouth Blues,* later called *Sugar Foot Stomp.* (They used to call him Louis Dipper-Mouth.)

Louis Panico who was with Isham Jones, and Paul Mares, of the Rhythm Kings, were both taking lessons from Joe then. Jelly Roll Morton was with the Rhythm Kings, too; Elmer Schoebel didn't join till a little later. Keppard's band was still going strong. He had Jimmy Noone on clarinet and Paul Barbarin, now with Luis Russell, on drums.

Around this time the Rhythm Kings started recording for Gennett, making numbers like *Tin Roof Blues, Bugle Call Rag,* and *Eccentric.* Joe also recorded for Gennett, making *Some Day, Sweetheart, Dipper*

Mouth Blues, and others. This was in 1921 or 1922. Joe had Johnny Dodds and Honore Dutrey with him then, but he replaced them with Jimmy Noone and Eddie Atkins. He had a contract with Gennett that would not permit him to make records for any other firm under his own name, and he claimed that Johnny and Dutrey played everything alike and would be dead give-aways. This caused a lot of friction in the band, for it was supposed to be a secret, but Johnny and Dutrey found out. Actually Joe was the give-away himself, for just like we can tell Louis on records today, they could tell Joe then. This trouble started the break-up of Joe's band.

Freddie Keppard was also having trouble. Freddie wanted to fire Paul Barbarin, but Jimmy Noone, who is Paul's brother-in-law, wouldn't stand for it, and quit, joining Charles Cooke's band at Harmon's Dreamland, Paul going back to New Orleans. This broke the band up and Bill Johnson went to Joe Oliver. In the meantime Joe had lost his band. They wanted to quit the Lincoln Gardens, but Joe didn't, so they went to Kelly's Stables without him. This was in 1923.

I had been playing trombone myself for a year, then, and Joe offered me a job, but I was afraid and refused. George Filhe was his trombonist; a wonderful musician and technician, but he couldn't get off. Joe also had Bob Shaffner, another wonderful trumpet player, with him, Charley Jackson on bass sax, and Lil Armstrong on piano. Louis was either with Erskine Tate or Fletcher Henderson at this time.

Then Paul Barbarin came back to Chicago, bringing Barney Bigard and Albert Nicholas with him. They started to work at the Lincoln Gardens, but were only there a little while when the place caught fire.

Joe took a band into the Plantation Cafe, while Louis played at the Sunset opposite with Carrol Dickerson. He had just returned from New York, where he had been with Fletcher Henderson, and was working with Erskine Tate's band at the Vendome Theatre as well.

A few of the boys you all know were beginning to come along now. Joe had with him at the plantation: Bert Cobb, tuba; Bob Shaffner, trumpet; Barney Bigard, tenor and clarinet; Albert Nicholas, alto and clarinet; Darnell Howard, alto; Bud Scott, guitar; Paul Barbarin, drums; Edward Ory, trombone; and Luis Russell, piano and arranger. Luis had come along from New Orleans with Barney and Nicholas. Joe, of course, was still playing trumpet with the band himself as well.

Bigard, Howard, and Nicholas were riots on saxes, Barney being considered the King of the tenor. Hawkins was with Fletcher Henderson, but was more or less unknown.

At the Sunset, Carrol had Earl Hines and Hamby on pianos; Louis and Shirley Clay, trumpets; Honore Dutrey, trombone; Dave Brown, Joe Walker, and Stumpy Evans, saxes and clarinets; Tubby Hall, drums; and Peter Briggs, tuba. As I have said, Louis was also working with Erskine Tate. It was quite common for the boys to double in this way. Jimmy Noone, for instance, was being featured with Cooke's Band at the Dreamland Ballroom, playing there from 8.00 P.M. to 12.00 P.M. but he also had a small combination of his own at the Apex Club to which he went on after. Freddie Keppard was still being featured with Cooke, too.

The Plantation closed soon after this, but Joe Oliver still kept his band together, with one or two alterations. Darnell Howard replaced Dave Brown, and Bob Shaffner was replaced by Tick Gray. Later still he replaced Howard with George James. At about this time Henry Allen, Jr., was the big noise in New Orleans, and Joe sent for him to come to Chicago. You will notice how nearly all the boys who have come to the front afterwards started with Joe.

Soon after the Plantation closed Joe left Chicago and went on tour. That was in 1925 or '26. He went to New York and filled an engagement there; then the band loafed for a bit and after a while broke up. Before this, however, Albert Nicholas had been replaced by Omer Simeon. After the break Nicholas and Howard went to China and the Duke took Bigard. He wanted Omer Simeon, also, but Omer preferred to go back to Chicago. Ory went back to Chicago also, but Luis Russell and Henry Allen stayed. The Duke picked up Braud at about this time, too; he had left Chicago in 1924 and had been around with Freddie Keppard, playing string bass and trombone.

Joe stayed in New York for quite a while, and did a lot of recording, but his band was shot to pieces. In the meantime Louis was causing a sensation at the Savoy Ballroom with Carrol Dickerson. Carrol had made quite a few alterations in his band. Tubby Hall, his drummer, had left him to go with Clarence Black and had been replaced by Zutie Singleton. Zutie had been in the Navy and had later played with Robicheaux at the Lyric Theatre in New Orleans.

The full personnel of Carrol's band then was: Louis and Homer Hopson, trumpets; Fred Robinson, trombone; Jimmie Strong, tenor; Bert Curry and Crawford Wetherington (now 1st alto with Mills' Blue Rhythm Band), altos; Prince, piano; Zutie, drums; Peck Carr, banjo; and Peter Briggs, bass. They cut every band that came to the Savoy including Fletcher Henderson and McKinney's Cotton Pickers. All they had to do was play *Savoy Blues, Some of These Days,* and the *St. Louis Blues* and the fight was over.

However, to return to Joe Oliver. The next time I saw him was in Houston, Texas. He had a good band then, but it broke up again soon after. Joe had had a lot of teeth pulled and just couldn't get started after it. He was never the same.

In the meantime Tommy Ladnier went away and came back a topnotcher. He joined Fletcher Henderson when Louis quit. Miff Mole was supposed to be the King of the trombone at that time; he and Jimmy Harrison. Teagarden was unheard of. Bix was coming strong, though. He lived not far away in the adjoining State of Indiana.

When the Savoy closed Louis took Carrol Dickerson's band back to New York where they opened at Connie's Inn as Louis Armstrong's Band. At the same time Louis was being featured on Broadway with the Hot Chocolates, making famous such numbers as *I Can't Give You Anything But Love* and *Ain't Misbehavin'.* The band broke up after about two years, and Louis left New York and went to California, passing through Chicago on his way. He came back the following year and organized another band, of which I was a member. We toured four or five months and then opened at the Suburban Gardens in New Orleans.

Oh boy! What a thrill. Ten thousand people met us at the station with eight bands. We were back home again in New Orleans after an absence of ten years, and stayed there for three months. We were broadcasting a lot of the time, and it is said that more people bought radios at that time than ever before. All the papers spoke of the boys who had gone to the big city and made good. Louis made the home in which he started playing a present of a fine radio and some instruments. He had a baseball team named after him—Armstrong's Secret Nine, and a cigar—the Armstrong Special.

After leaving New Orleans we toured the Southern States, playing six weeks on the RKO circuit, and then touring again, mostly dance dates. Then back to New York again.

We made two shorts for Paramount there—*You Rascal, You,* and *Rhapsody in Black and Blue,* and played the Lafayette Theatre. Then, when Louis returned to New York, we were disbanded.

I shall never forget the time in Boston when we played against Fletcher Henderson and the Casa Loma Orchestra, the latter having just whipped McKinney's Cotton Pickers in Philadelphia. Louis made 260 high C's and finished on top F—and the fight was over.

The personnel of Louis' band at this time was: George James, Al. Washington, and Lester Boone, reeds; Randolph, Louis, and myself, brass; John Lindsey, bass; Tubby Hall, drums; Charlie Alexander, piano; and Mike McKendrick, guitar.

I started off to tell you about Joe Oliver, but seem to have managed to drag in Louis and all the other New Orleans boys, but that's just the way I run on when I get talking about the old days and some of the grand old-timers.

The New Orleans Rhythm Kings

GEORGE BEALL

from *Swing Music*

The Chicago story, on the white side, which most of us pick up with the Austin High Gang and the Teschmaker records, really begins with the New Orleans Rhythm Kings, an orchestra which set the style for the jazz-struck kids who are today the core of the non-commercial white bands. The British Swing Music *was rhapsodizing over this historic band in 1935, and the article by George Beall which follows appeared in its pages. There is considerable talk today about the Negro musicians of the post-war (I) era and this has overflowed into an interest in the New Orleans Rhythm Kings, but the records Mares and Rapollo made are harder to obtain in the original or in reissue than those of King Oliver, Freddie Keppard, or Jelly Roll. Perhaps the re-publication of George Beall's study will help in arousing enough interest so that some enterprising record company will begin to make the NORK recordings available. (ED.)*

IN the fabulous early post-war days of jazz, Chicago was perhaps the first large city in America north of the Mason-Dixon line to have a taste of that strange new music from the deep South. Many people, hearing a jazz band for the first time, deemed the performers either drunk or crazy, but the visits of Tom Brown's Jazz Band, the Original Dixieland Jazz Band, and Earl Fuller's Jazz Band (which, though not a southern band, had early discovered and adopted the New Orleans style) to that city created such interest in the music that booking agents were working overtime trying to import enough musicians from New Orleans to fill the demand. Thus, from New Orleans to Chicago a steady influx of men possessed of amazing talent and an equally amazing inability

78

to read music, soon took place. To a woman, however, belongs the credit for the purely fortuitous formation of one of the greatest bands of all time, the band whose place is on the same level in jazz history with the Original Dixieland Jazz Band—the Friar's Inn Society Orchestra. She is Bee Palmer, one of the earliest forerunners of our modern torch singers and a famous variety performer, known at that time all over the South and Middle West. It was her custom to take a road show out of New Orleans to various cities throughout those sections; which show invariably featured a small band playing in the then new and strange New Orleans jazz style. When the peak of the first enthusiasm for New Orleans jazz was reached in Chicago, about 1920, she was booked in there with her customary aggregation, special emphasis having been put by the agents on the necessity of having a good jazz band along with her. Several promising young fellows playing about in New Orleans attracted her attention and she persuaded them to join her troupe for the invasion of the hinterland. These men were Paul Mares, Leon Rapollo, George Brunies, one of a family of nine or ten members, all musicians, and Arnold Loyacano, who had already visited Chicago's land of promise with Tom Brown's Jazz Band several years before.

When Bee Palmer's show opened in Chicago it was a terrific sensation, and the small band of five or six members playing with the troupe was responsible for most of the attention attracted by the performances. After the show's run was over the musicians decided to avail themselves of one of the many attractive offers they had received. The management at the Friar's Inn, well-known Chicago night spot, was very anxious to feature this new type of music, and offered what seemed princely wages to these young musicians, with the stipulation that they augment their group to eight or nine members, the number fitting for a band in so well-known and high-class a resort. Mares and Rapollo had become fairly well acquainted in musicians' circles in Chicago and knew they could add the necessary number of men who would fit, without any trouble. A young pianist named Elmer Schoebel from Champaign, Illinois, who had been making a name for himself accompanying vocalists in cafes here and there in Chicago, was added to the group. Three other promising young natives of Chicago, Jack Pettis, sax; Frank Snyder, drums; Lew Black, banjo, soon found berths in the outfit and the band was ready to begin making history at the Friar's Inn. This first combination was composed of the following: Mares, trumpet; Brunies, trombone; Rapollo and Pettis, reeds; Schoebel, piano; Black, banjo; Snyder, drums; and Loyacano, bass.

In no time the fame of the wonderful new band in Chicago had spread well beyond the confines of that city, and visiting musicians invariably hastened to the Friar's Inn to hear the band go through its strange but effective paces. At times we feel the management must have wondered whether or not the band was really a good thing for them, as the musicians and fans who jammed the place from 7 P.M. to 7 A.M. kept out no small portion of a more monied clientele. However, whether through the altruism of the owners or through some obscure prescience on their part that this group would go down in history, the band remained. Within a few months after its formation, two important changes in the personnel took place. Loyacano having been taken sick, Steve Brown, that tremendous string-bass slapper, was persuaded to leave his job at Alterni's on the South side of Chicago and join the band, a move they had tried unsuccessfully to induce him to make before.

With the replacement of Snyder by Ben Pollack, a hard-hitting local drummer, the rhythm section stood at least on a par with the remainder of the band. This was the formation that was to achieve deathless fame among the record collectors. They featured in their performances principally numbers composed by the band or its individual members. These are almost legion; one could enumerate almost endlessly the compositions by Schoebel alone. For a number of years he had vainly tried to interest publishers in his tunes, then after they were featured by the Friar's Inn Orchestra, such was the immediate and commanding prestige of the band, he was swamped with offers from the very firms that had unfailingly rejected his efforts in the past. He was offered a large salary by one publishing house and was frequently requested to write topical numbers by publishers eager to capitalize outstanding incidents of the day. At the time of the sensational House of David scandal in the Middle West, a representative of the Robbins firm, anxious to be first with a comedy number (of the type popular in the early twenties) based on this spicy front-page news, made a dash from New York to Chicago to enlist Schoebel's services. He found him in a cafe with Brown and Meyers, Schoebel's lyric-writing partner. Within an hour the famous *House of David Blues* had taken shape, and Robbins scored an immense triumph, anticipating the field by several weeks with this number.

Although the other members of the band possessed their share of talent in composition, as, for instance, Mares' *Blues in E Flat*, Schoebel not only dominated the band in this particular line, but in another and more important way. It was principally due to his ideas and influence that the original New Orleans style practised by the band gave way to a newer, more advanced style that was to have an incalculable effect on the future development of jazz. At first their method of attack was purely gut-bucket; every man for himself and Heaven help the fellow with poor lungs or weak arms. Schoebel it was, however, who began to alter this style by pre-determining definite parts for each man to play; by the introduction of patterns, simple though they were, and a more even rhythmic background. Arrangements were, of course, impossible as we know them today, if only from the fact that the most important members of the melody section, Mares, Rapollo and Brunies, could not read music. Schoebel nevertheless spent numberless rehearsals in drilling these men in parts which we might call arranged, although not a note of music was set down for them and which the performers had perforce to learn by sheer memory.

This evolution of their style resulted in even greater popularity for the band and even greater conviction on the part of the management of the Inn that they were operating a musicians' club. The late Don Murray once described his impression of Rapollo in a way that recalls much of the atmosphere of that heyday of the giants of early jazz. Don, who as a schoolboy in Chicago made a home away from home of Friar's Inn, said: "I used to get a terrific sock out of Rapollo riding high on his clarinet, with one foot braced high up on a pillar alongside the stand and so full of marihuana he could scarcely move out of his chair at the finish of a set." Naturally the band received countless offers to go elsewhere, some of which at figures so stupendous to these inexperienced youngsters that they passed them up as hoaxes. The only trips away from Chicago they made were to Richmond, Indiana, to record for the Gennett Company. After nearly three years of such unprecedented acclaim the group entered the period of disintegration which was climaxed in 1925. Rapollo's addiction to narcotics made him less reliable, and finally in 1924 Brown left the band to go into the Midway Gardens Orchestra, where Schoebel soon joined him. Although Schoebel was soon replaced by Mel Stitzel, the men found it impossible to fill Brown's place satisfactorily and for a while he played in both the Friar's Inn band and the Midway Gardens Orchestra, five hours a night in each. He was unable to go this pace for long, however, and Mares sent to New Orleans for Chink Martin to play bass with the band regularly. This group seemed to lack some of the punch of its predecessor, and although the later records by the New Orleans Rhythm Kings made by this set-up does not show this falling off, their popularity was on the wane. Then Pettis left to join Ben Bernie and Brunies went over to Ted Lewis. Although Volly Devoe, who had occasionally augmented the band, took Pettis' place, the end had come. In the early part of 1925 Rapollo was confined to a sanatorium, his mind a wreck from the weed, and the remainder of the unit went to Indianapolis, where they eventually disbanded. Mares and Martin returned to New Orleans, giving up music for the time; Black, Devoe and Stitzel dropped into comparative obscurity. Pollack returned to Chicago, where he persuaded Benny Goodman to leave the Midway Gardens Orchestra and go with him into the Southmore Hotel, along with Sterling Bowes, and soon after, Ray Bauduc. In just such a prosaic way, in sharp contrast to their sudden leap to fame, gradually ended the existence of the greatest hot band of the early twenties, just at the time when the developments they had pioneered were sweeping the country.

The records by the Friar's Inn Orchestra were all made for Gennett, that company which with amazing perspicacity or sheer good luck, had under contract at one time or another nearly all the classic combinations of the period. As a consequence, when it failed in 1929, a great part of the most interesting discs issued during that time were made unavailable, and today a clean copy of any Gennett by the outstanding hot men of the years 1921 to 1926 is almost priceless. In spite of the tremendous sale of the Friar's Inn Gennetts, they are exceedingly rare outside the collectors' realm. In some ten or twelve years of collecting records, during the course of which I have examined probably one hundred and fifty or two hundred thousand second-hand or discarded records, I have come upon only four Gennetts by the Friar's Inn Orchestra in this usually fruitful source.

Most of the numbers recorded by the band were their own compositions, such as *Tin Roof Blues, Farewell Blues, Bugle Call Blues, Milen-*

berg Joys, That's a Plenty; tunes which immediately became tremendously popular and have remained so down to this day. Several of these discs sold as many as two hundred thousand copies, most of which went into the hands of musicians or fans, where they have remained. For the age of these relics of a classic day, they are extraordinary. Many of them could compete as to genuine hot execution with a large proportion of later records by bands supposedly advanced in technique and ideas. *That's a Plenty* and *Tin Roof Blues,* recorded in 1922, is one of the best examples of the output of this group. Mares' trumpet playing is tremendous: his attack is spirited, his tone round and full; his ideas, though hackneyed now through too assiduous emulation by· others, are succinctly and forcefully presented. Rapollo, perhaps the most advanced musician in the group, plays with great feeling; his tone, detached and nostalgic, never fails to produce emotional response in his auditors. Brunies' part on trombone is rather ambiguous; at times he carries the melody, then again, somewhat in the Dixieland tradition, he supports the rhythm section. On the records, this latter portion of the band seems to lack depth, due to the fact that Brown's puissant bass would not record, the usual thing in those days. He is present on most of the records, however, taking part in the recording session although the men know his part would not be directly apparent on the discs, for the sole purpose of keeping the rhythm section at the peak of its power. Schoebel, Black and Pollack appear to good advantage, maintaining an even rhythmic flow amazing in that day. Black and Pollack are particularly effective on *Bugle Call Blues;* Lew sounds like a one-man rhythm section and takes the greater part of the credit for the buoyant spirit of this disc. *Tiger Rag, Shimmeshawabble* and *Farewell Blues* all show the band's great power and represent one of the most important milestones in the evolution of jazz.

In connection with the records by the Friar's Inn Orchestra, there is a story behind their use of two different recording names. Soon after the group gained its first great popularity, they were approached by Husk O'Hare who offered them a proposal regarding recording. O'Hare was a native of Chicago, notorious for sharp practices, and the occasional leader of a second-rate band. In discussing the matter of making records with the Friar's Ínn boys, O'Hare, who had discovered that the Gennett Company was eager to have them under contract, told them that he was a stockholder in the Gennett Company and could arrange very favorable terms for them. They accepted his offer, even giving him the responsibility of handling all details with the Gennett people. O'Hare, always a seeker of cheap publicity, so arranged matters that the sides recorded in their first session were released as "The Friar's Inn Society Orchestra, direction of Husk O'Hare." The band was woefully taken in through their ignorance of O'Hare's true status (he owned no stock in the Gennett Company and had represented himself as the leader of the band to the company) and of the fact that the Gennett Company had been on the point of making them a direct offer. Consequently, on the following records they cut for Gennett, they had themselves named "New Orleans Rhythm Kings, formerly Friar's Inn Orchestra."

Looked at critically, all these records must necessarily be examined in the light of the period in which they were made. To compare them, making no such allowances, with present day discs by Ellington, Henderson or Goodman is patently ridiculous. In their own way they are as important as any of these. Although these records appeared just a year or two after the Original Dixieland reached its peak, yet the strides made by the Friar's Inn band were tremendous, heralding the beginning of that brief era of rapid development that crystallized in the form of the modern jazz style sometime about 1926. The Friar's Inn men added variety to the monotonous renditions of the Dixieland by the inclusion of fairly extended solos, as well as less rigid adherence to one or two simple variations on the basic theme. Arranging began to make an appearance, the band as a unit displayed greater balance. In a comparison for example of *Bluin' the Blues* or *At the Jazz Band Ball* by the Original Dixieland and *Tin Roof Blues* or *Farewell Blues* by the Friar's Inn, one cannot help feeling with all due respect to the Dixieland, its sincerity and spirit, that the junior group possessed infinitely greater originality and imaginativeness. In the discs by the Dixieland, we find the same *ad lib* phrase repeated again and again, giving weight to the impression that the performer intends to convey his idea by sheer repetition. True, the genuine spirit is always present in the Original Dixieland's efforts, but the expression seems sadly lacking. The Friar's Inn band is not hampered by any such rigid repetitions in expressing its ideas; a telling phrase introduced by one soloist is repeated with variations by another, harmonies and key changes add to the pleasing effect of their output. The rhythm section provided an even foundation for the building up and display of the ensemble and solo parts, a tremendous advance over the atmosphere of conflict and jerkiness generally produced by the Original Dixieland. However, the greater feature of interest of these ancient records is the fact that they represent such a definite stage in the development of jazz, as well as that they are the only tangible criteria of an organization which yet remains almost as famous as it was in its great days.

Chicago in these later days of the Friar's Inn Orchestra, had already begun to supersede New Orleans as the capital of jazz. So many men, even at that time well-known or later to become famous, were playing in and about Chicago that one could scarcely encounter a band anywhere in that City whose personnel did not include some name now known to all admirers of jazz. Armstrong, Goodman, Bix, Spanier, Carmichael, Joe Oliver, Condon, Sullivan, Mannone, Krupa and many others were busily engaged according to their various blowings and poundings, in making Chicago famous as the locale of an amazing concentration of great hot musicians. It is no mean tribute to the position of the Friar's Inn band in jazz history, that contemporary opinion among the musicians in Chicago rated them highest. Their fresh style, offering much greater opportunity to their admirers and imitators, marked the first great departure from the early stages of jazz. They were the first hot band to use as many as eight or nine pieces, including a four piece rhythm section; the fact that other hot combinations clung stubbornly to the older Dixieland conception of a five-piece outfit, makes it apparent that this was a radical departure. Although individuals contemporary with the Friar's Inn band, notably King Oliver, have had as great influence though of a different sort, on the future of jazz, the influence of these was not as immediate nor so widely appreciated. In a way, the advances they pioneered worked to their eventual downfall. As arranging developed from the start they gave it, the Friar's Inn Band found it more and more difficult, as did most of the New Orleans veterans, through the trouble written parts caused them. Eventually, the musician unable to read music was completely in the discard simply because of the growing complexity of written arrangements. Nevertheless, this group of men has held place through the years with the Original Dixieland as one of the greatest of the classic hot bands, and their fame today is as widely scattered as that of the earlier group. Now that it is assured that the priceless discs made by the Friar's Inn Society Orchestra will again be available to the interested public, through the foresight and progressive attitude of the Brunswick company,[1] as well as through the efforts of several individuals, collectors unfamiliar with their work will have the long-sought opportunity of acquainting themselves with these almost fabulous figures of jazz history.

[1] This, unfortunately for us, referred to British Brunswick. (ED.)

Jazz Pre-History—and Bunk Johnson

MORROE BERGER

Jazz criticism, which began as an amateur's field with the exploratory writings of Robert Goffin and Hugues Panassié in the early Thirties, has become the highly specialized province of social scientists. Whether this will lead to a scattering of the dry dust of the academy on a fresh and unspoiled field is a moot question. But the writings of Morroe Berger certainly do not fall into the pedantic category. He is a Columbia University Fellow in Sociology, one of the more enduring prodigies of the Department, who is preparing a doctoral thesis on jazz.

In his successful attempt at applying the sociological approach to jazz. Berger has added to the sum total of our knowledge, brushed away many of the synthetic cobwebs manufactured by the jazz obscurantists, and begun the tremendous task of placing jazz in a proper perspective. The controversial pages which follow are from the introduction to his study on the diffusion of jazz, a work now in progress. (ED.)

AFTER Jelly Roll Morton's rediscovery in 1939 it began to appear that every collector had in his pocket (next to the manuscript of the definitive study of jazz) at least one great musician who had played with Buddy Bolden or King Oliver or Fate Marable, and who was now all but entirely forgotten.

The biggest rediscovery in the jazz world, however, has been the revival not of a particular musician, but of the jazz music of New Orleans as played around the turn of the century. Early jazz never was recorded for sale, although it almost was in 1916, when Victor offered to record the music of Freddie Keppard and his Original Creole Band. But the great trumpeter turned down the proposition because he didn't want the band's stuff to be stolen by others.[1] It has been only very recently, since the formation of the Kid Ory band (with Mutt Carey and others) in Los Angeles and the Bunk Johnson band in New York, that we have been able to get a good idea of the vitality and superior quality of this early jazz. A good deal of it has been put on records by Bunk and Kid Ory, Alphonse Picou, Big Eye Louis Nelson, Pete Bocage, and others.

The recovery of early jazz has centered around the reappearance of Bunk Johnson in the musical world. Bunk was no ordinary jazzman dug out of obscurity, for he was said to be the oldest living jazz pioneer, and he himself claimed to have "started jazz" in New Orleans ("or any place else") with Buddy Bolden.[2] Bunk's discovery goes back to a remark of Louis Armstrong's in 1938. William Russell, then gathering material for his contribution to *Jazzmen,* had asked the great man some questions. Louis, apparently no more concerned about jazz history than most other musicians, suggested that Russell look up Bunk Johnson, who would know all about the early days of jazz in New Orleans.[3]

With the aid of the local post office, Russell located Bunk in New Iberia, a small Louisiana town west of New Orleans. Then Russell began a fruitful correspondence with Bunk, parts of which enlivened the opening pages of *Jazzmen.* Bunk often claimed that he could play again if only he had a good set of teeth. Some of the *Jazzmen* contributors, skeptical of the old man's claims but wanting to help him anyway, raised the money for a set of plates that Leonard Bechet, Sidney's brother, made for Bunk.

Collectors now began to make the pilgrimage to New Iberia to see Bunk and talk with him about jazz. Some visitors made a few talking records, but with poor facilities. In the spring of 1942, two groups of collectors, from the East and West Coasts, converged upon Bunk at about the same time to record him with a band of veteran New Orleans musicians. The West Coast group issued the recordings on the *Jazz Man* label, but again the recording equipment was inferior. Later in

---

[1] *Jazzmen,* ed. by Charles Edward Smith and Frederic Ramsey, Jr. (N. Y., 1939) p. 22.
[2] Ibid., after title page.
[3] I am indebted to Eugene Williams for help in obtaining these facts about Bunk Johnson's recent career.

the summer of 1942, Eugene Williams, one of Bunk's East Coast admirers, made some records of Bunk that were technically better than
the others, and released them on the *Jazz Information* label.

Not long after these two recording dates Bunk was called to San
Francisco, where he played to illustrate a lecture on jazz before a
highbrow museum audience. In San Francisco, living with one of his
collector friends, Bunk did no more than play a few concerts and
Sunday afternoon sessions. He also made some records (never released)
with those members of the Lu Watters band who had survived the
draft. Early in 1944 Bunk returned to New Iberia. Shortly afterward he
reappeared in San Francisco, hoping to play regularly with some of
the Lu Watters men; but union trouble over mixed white and Negro
bands spiked that plan.

For a brief period in 1944 Bunk tried Los Angeles. He recorded with
a pickup band, but these transcriptions were never placed on sale, since
they were made for the exclusive use of broadcasters. After returning
once more to New Iberia, Bunk recorded for William Russell in 1944,
on the *American Music* label. In the fall, the National Jazz Foundation,
organized in New Orleans to preserve and foster jazz, sponsored a
concert there. Bunk played a wagon advertising the concert in the city
streets, but did not play at the concert itself. A few months later, in
January of 1945, *Esquire* sponsored a similar concert in New Orleans,
at which Bunk broadcast one number with Louis Armstrong and then
played (but did not broadcast) with his own band.

Up to this time Bunk was but slightly known to jazz followers. His
records were not a trustworthy guide to his musicianship, and few had
heard him in person. In the spring of 1945 Bunk made his memorable
debut in New York at a Sunday afternoon jam session at Jimmy Ryan's
on 52nd Street. On this trip to New York Bunk recorded with Sidney
Bechet for *Blue Note,* but apparently the plans to release these records
have been abandoned. With Bechet, Bunk played in Boston for about
a month, but the association (in some respects a jazz lover's dream combination, like Sidney and Louis Armstrong at the session resulting in
the Decca *New Orleans Jazz* album) was cut short by disagreement
between them on musical matters.

On his return to New York Bunk opened at the Stuyvesant Casino,
in September of 1945, playing with Jim Robinson, George Lewis, Baby

Dodds, Alcide Pavageau (Slow Drag), Lawrence Marrero, and Alton Purnell. Now the public got its chance to hear Bunk and his kind of jazz under reasonably favorable circumstances. The impact of the outfit was like that of a bombshell. Night after night New Yorkers could step into a hall and hear superb jazz, for in sustained playing Bunk exceeded the promise indicated on his records. Jim Robinson on trombone made a great impression too, fulfilling the expectations aroused by his powerful work on the *Delta* records with Alphonse Picou, Big Eye Louis Nelson and Kid Rena.

In January of 1946 Bunk and the band returned to New Orleans. Most of them came back with Bunk for another engagement at the Casino in the spring, but this was short-lived, ending in a few weeks. Bunk again went home. At this writing Bunk would like to form another band, one that he can direct without the distracting influence of men who cannot or will not do what he wants. There are also some movie offers hanging fire, and Bunk would like nothing better than to tap the Hollywood till.

The jazz that Bunk Johnson first heard when he tagged after the great players of the day hardly touched any but a Negro audience. Jazz before Storyville was not so closely identified with white men's vice as it later became. It was always the music of the lower classes, however, so that when Storyville came into official existence in 1897, Negro jazzmen found a great number of new opportunities, since the white man wanted this uninhibited low-down music to provide the background for the unconventional play of the sporting houses. The popularity of Negro jazz had opened up a wide area, even before Storyville, in which Negroes could obtain employment in a "clean occupation" (though some may think the name inappropriate for the kind of music played and the joints that featured it). Harry Dial, a Negro drummer who has played with a variety of bands, has remarked that music is "a great business and a great trade. It's the only other profession, outside of sports, where an uneducated man can earn a swell living." [4] This enthusiastic judgment certainly must have applied more to the situation around 1900 than it does to present-day conditions.

[4] "Drums on the Mississippi," *The Jazz Record,* Sept. 1946, p. 9.

New Orleans jazzmen of Bunk's time (his *first* career, that is) did not live apart from their audience. Many players held other jobs that brought them into the life of the community. They lived with their neighbors, played and drank with them; they were not a class apart, seen only when performing. During the Nineteen Twenties too there was relatively little separation between performer and listener, especially when compared with the gap that is apparent today in the contempt many name band leaders and musicians have for the teen-agers and moon-struck older people who idolize them. This close community of feeling between the players and their audience had a fruitful mutual effect. The audience could treat the players like human beings, and the players could continue to draw their inspiration from contact with an audience that liked and responded to things the musicians themselves favored.

Without formal training, the Negroes of New Orleans developed a kind of music that was to become recognized, after decades of disparagement, as a superb, unique American contribution to the world's musical heritage. America's greatest music was thus created by its least-honored and most-exploited sons and daughters, not in the conservatories and similar centers of cultural embalming. Of this development, Samuel I. Hayakawa, an American student of language and a jazz lover, has noted four interesting aspects: [5] 1) The Negroes tried to reproduce with instruments the styles and techniques of their earlier vocal music. 2) Early players, not formally educated in music, were not impeded by tradition; they tried for all sorts of effects and thereby considerably extended the range of their instruments. 3) They did not follow the late European tradition of separation of the performer and composer. In their improvisations the New Orleans Negroes played and composed at the same time. 4) The music they created as a development of folk music, but now for the first time this kind of music had the advantage of being produced with modern instruments.

The spread of New Orleans jazz is usually said to have begun between 1900 and 1918. There is, however, ample evidence that its diffusion had already occurred at least a quarter-century before 1900, for in 1876 Lafcadio Hearn contributed an article on "Levee Life" to *The*

[5] "Reflections on the History of Jazz," a reprint of a lecture given on March 17, 1945, obtainable from Dr. Hayakawa at the Illinois Institute of Technology, Chicago.

Commercial, a Cincinnati publication,[6] in which he wrote of Negro life at the Cincinnati docks, of the dancing and singing of the dock-workers, the sailors and their women. They did the Virginia reel, slow and fast quadrilles and the shimmy. Their songs, as is characteristic of early Negro music, were about their work and play, and some of them Hearn called (with not the slightest intention to disapprove) immoral and profane. The influence of New Orleans is obvious in many of the songs Hearn printed. One song refers to a man from New Orleans, another to a shipping company called the New Orleans Line, and a third tells about the singer's plan to return to New Orleans. The levee dance halls and drinking places were most crowded, Hearn reported, when the New Orleans boats were in port (he mentioned especially a joint run by one Ryan, a name still to be respected in jazz). The music itself Hearn described in such terms as "slow and sweet," "plaintive," "lengthy chants," "sonorous and regularly slow." Obviously this is the blues, the contribution to jazz made by Negroes of slave origin.

Another important strain of jazz appeared in Cincinnati in the music that was probably played to accompany the slow and fast quadrilles. This was the contribution of the heritage of the *hommes libres de couleur,* the "free men of color" who had thrived under the liberal traditions of the French in Louisiana. Theirs was a more traditional ingredient compounded in jazz, more refined and more European than the others. Jazzmen like Picou, Nelson, Perez, Baquet and Bocage are of Creole-free Negro origin, but in them the fusion of the two strains in jazz was virtually completed. But the generation before them, their own teachers, for example, had been brought up in the classical tra-dition. When we reach Sidney Bechet the fusion is complete, for though he is of free-Negro origin Bechet was not given a formal musical edu-cation; yet he combines the lyricism of the Creole tradition with the abandon and power of the slave-Negro strain in jazz.[7]

Jazz, being the music of an exploited people, did not meet with the approval of the guardians of public taste. When jazz became further smirched by its association with vice in Storyville during the 1890's, the

[6] Reprinted in Lafcadio Hearn, *An American Miscellany,* ed. by Albert Mordell, V. 1 (N. Y., 1924), pp. 147-170.
[7] Good examples of these two strains may be heard on Bechet's *Egyptian Fantasy* (Victor 27337), which incidentally is a favorite of Big Eye Louis Nelson, and on *Dear Old Southland* (Blue Note 13), as well as on Jelly Roll Morton's *The Crave* (General 4003).

respectable classes outlawed it entirely. They liked Negro slave songs, but not Negro jazz, which they considered base, as one lady folklorist wrote in 1919.[8] In Chicago during the Prohibition era the identification of jazz with vice and crime reached a peak. Despite such eminently respectable jazz organizations as the National Jazz Foundation, which has the blessing of the New Orleans Chamber of Commerce, people still persist in thinking jazz immoral. As late as the winter of 1946, after years of playing at New York's Town Hall, Eddie Condon was refused permission to bring his band to Constitution Hall in Washington, D. C., owned by the Daughters of the American Revolution. The managing director feared "the type of audience" that follows jazz bands, and expected that it "may be very destructive."[9] Obviously the representative of the ladies thought that Condon might draw an audience similar to the one that punished the Paramount Theatre in New York when Benny Goodman brought his big band there in 1937. Actually the Condon concert would undoubtedly have been attended by some of Washington's leading administrators and intellectuals—so far had jazz come since its Red Light days.

Even among tradition-bound Negro musicians, such as Will Handy, jazz was something to be avoided. As he relates,[10] he "took up with low forms hesitantly . . . wondering if they were quite the thing." While playing at a Negro dance in a small Mississippi town in 1903, Handy first began to realize the appeal of jazz when a few local boys got up and played a new kind of rhythm for which the audience went wild. They showered the amateurs with more money than Handy and his professionals were paid for the job. "Then," says Handy, "I saw the beauty of primitive music. It touched the spot . . . Folks would pay money for it." As the music gained popularity, he began to write down the tunes he heard, for his idea of "what constitutes music was changed by the sight of that silver money cascading around the splay feet of a Mississippi string band."

Even before the beginning of the great trek to Chicago the influence of New Orleans music was felt in the North as minstrels, travelling

8 Emily Le Jeune, *Creole Folk Songs, Louisiana Historical Quarterly*, October 1919, Vol. 2, No. 4, pp. 454-55.
9 *New York Times*, February 21, 1946, page 23.
10 *Father of the Blues* (N. Y., 1941), pp. 75-78.

bands and circus and carnival musicians were heard in various parts of the country. At least as early as 1913 (and probably earlier) New York and other large cities were hit by a dance craze. What drew most of the attention was the kind of dancing, not the music; but the feel of jazz had certainly penetrated. A few years later the music became better known as ragtime or jazz, and then it began to draw its share of criticism for leading to juvenile delinquency, drinking, vice, disobedience of parents, increased divorces and short tempers. The object of these attacks was called "jazz," but it was the derivatives of jazz rather than genuine New Orleans music that the irate citizens heard. Few observers knew this at the time, but the late James Weldon Johnson, Negro writer and fighter for Negro rights, was perfectly aware of the big steal already in progress by which copyists gained fame and money by using jazz materials, while the great Negro jazzmen died unknown in poverty. In his *Autobiography of an Ex-Colored Man,* published anonymously in 1912, Johnson pointed out this development, and, referring to the representatives of "serious" music, he wrote: "American musicians, instead of investigating rag-time, attempt to ignore it, or dismiss it with a contemptuous word. But that has always been the course of scholasticism in every branch of art . . ." [11]

Jazz music and jazzmen have been gaining recognition in recent years, in contrast to their previous treatment by the public and our cultural leaders. Even Negro scholars who look into every obscure corner for some evidence of a Negro contribution to American life have not considered jazz worthy of a place among the notable achievements of Negroes. Although James Weldon Johnson in 1912 claimed that "ragtime" was one of the four greatest Negro cultural developments (the cakewalk was another), scholars after him have not been so aware of the greatness of jazz. Benjamin Brawley, a leading chronicler of Negro life, does not mention jazz even once in three of his best known books on Negro culture. [12] Dr. W. E. Burghardt Du Bois, one of the most prominent of Negro intellectual leaders, does not mention jazz

[11] 1927 edition (N. Y.), page 100.
[12] *Short History of the American Negro* (Revised) (N. Y., 1919). *The Negro in Literature and Art* (N. Y., 1918). *Negro Builders and Heroes* (Chapel Hill, 1937).

in a discussion of Negro contributions to American music.[13] Edwin R. Embree, however, in *Brown America,* does devote a few words to Negro jazz.[14] Few other writers in this field reveal any understanding of jazz; some are impressed more with the triumphs of the big successful Negro musicians such as Henderson, Ellington and Calloway, than with the pioneers and perpetuators of the jazz tradition, who are not so well known to the general public.

The recognition that Bunk Johnson and other older jazzmen have attained in the last few years is a good sign for jazz. Too often great jazzmen were dead for many years before their names became big enough to bring substantial returns in the glory and cold cash that are so abundant in the American entertainment business. King Oliver, dying in poverty in 1938, wasn't helped much by the fact that seven years later a record collector paid out one hundred and sixty dollars for a new copy of *Chimes Blues* on the original label. Thus far, unfortunately, the growth of the popularity of jazz has benefited jazz experts, concert promoters and record dealers more than it has the musicians.

While Bunk's recognition is certainly deserved, a small cult within the jazz cult has formed which builds him up as the greatest jazz player that is or was, the only one who plays the real stuff, except for the men in the Kid Ory and Lu Watters bands. Fed by Bunk's vaunted fertile memory, this group by implication dwarfs most other living jazz players who, after all, are pretty good too. This cultish activity is in some respects as offensive as *Esquire's* meaningless annual poll of the experts to select the All-American team for jazz. Though the two groups are widely separated in musical taste, actually the holier-than-thous of the Bunk-Kid Ory mob are quite like the "advanced-jazz" Esquire crowd. Both sides are addicted to pointing out the "best" and to ignoring a world of jazzmen who continue to take a beating so that they can play the jazz they like and play it as well as the glorified "bests" of each group.

When Jelly Roll Morton said he invented jazz in 1902, no one believed him. Jazz players are not always to be taken at their word about jazz history, and it is the responsibility of writers on jazz to avoid repeating all that they hear. The process by which writers convert memo-

[13] *Black Folk Then and Now* (N. Y., 1939), p. 218.
[14] (N. Y., 1937), pp. 243-4.

ries into learned historical treatises on jazz yields some notions that cannot always be sensibly defended. Bunk indulged in some personal press-agenting—no one can object very strenuously to that, because Bunk is a fine musician who is only now coming near to getting his due. But the chroniclers of jazz must exercise more selectivity if there is to be any trustworthy historical literature on the subject.

The beginning of the Bunk legend came in 1939, with the publication of *Jazzmen,* which at last provided excellent jazz history and criticism from a sympathetic viewpoint. This book has deservedly become a reference work for the careers of the musicians who made and still make jazz history. Like so many other monumental works, however, it has been received too readily as the last word. This is easy to understand, for the subject is one whose exact origins are obscure, and the evidence upon them is difficult to obtain. It is no wonder, then, that people have been happy to use it as authentic history—there is still so little else to rely upon.

It was in accepting Bunk's word so uncritically that some writers of *Jazzmen* made their greatest error. Bunk's motive, entirely understandable, was too exclusively the exaltation of his own role in jazz. His aim was obviously to reveal himself as the first of the jazz players in New Orleans, and certainly the oldest living pioneer. At times he seemed willing to concede he had predecessors, but all of them were dead. In a series of talks this writer had a few years ago in New Orleans with some of the oldest living jazz musicians, views on jazz history were turned up that didn't conform entirely to Bunk's story.

According to Bunk, he joined the Buddy Bolden band in 1895. This statement from memory was made in 1938, about an event that was supposed to have taken place more than forty years before, yet the writers seem to have made no effort to check the claim. They accepted it readily in spite of the lack of evidence that New Orleans bands, especially at that point in the development of jazz, had two cornetists as a regular practice. There is, on the other hand, considerable evidence in the photographs of the period and in the memories of other jazzmen such as Big Eye Louis Nelson and Alphonse Picou that the jazz band did not as a rule have two cornetists. The failure of Bunk's story to fit other apparent facts led to an interesting manipulation of dates in *Jazzmen.* The picture of the Bolden band reprinted in it does not include Bunk; but Bunk claims he joined it in 1895; hence the picture is captioned: "Kid Bolden's Band Before 1895." Nelson and Picou, however, both recall that the band shown above this caption played not in 1895 but almost a decade later.

In the hands of the jazz critics a simple statement like Bunk's can be made the basis for elaborate theories about the nature of early New Orleans jazz. Some writers have actually done so. Robert Goffin, accepting Bunk's statement that he joined Bolden in 1895, remarked concerning the addition of a second cornetist to the Bolden Band: "Thus came into being the classical form of the New Orleans band." [15] Two years later he indicated that he suspected some of Bunk's statements on this point.[16] Ernest Borneman, an anthropologist who has tried to apply scientific method to the study of jazz, wrote a series of articles in *The Record Changer* (collected in a pamphlet) in which he referred to the "greatest New Orleans tradition of contrapuntal cornet duets (Bolden-Johnson, Oliver-Armstrong) . . ." [17] It is difficult to find ample justification for such categorical pronouncements.

In emphasizing Bunk's position in jazz history the members of Bunk's admiration society naturally ignore that of early jazzmen who have some claims of their own. Alphonse Picou, for example, told me that he played clarinet in the "District" in 1894, at the age of 16. "I was so young they had to take me in through the side door, 'cause it was against the law. But I made the girls kick up all right." Picou claims he organized a jazz band in 1896. It was a seven-piece group called the Independent Band, and it played frequently at Hope's Hall.

Louis Nelson began to play jazz clarinet around 1897, after having played the accordion and guitar. Manuel Perez played cornet around the same time. Although he told me in 1943 that he could play again if he had a good set of teeth ("If Bunk can do it, so can I."), he has since become very ill and uncommunicative. All three of these pioneers claim they played at the same time Buddy Bolden did, or before him. Bolden, however, is usually placed first, even earlier than 1895. The 'reason for this antedating appears to be Bunk's claim, accepted by jazz historians without enough warrant, that he joined Bolden in 1895. Picou, Nelson

[15] *Jazz* (N. Y., 1944), p. 35.
[16] " 'Big Eye' Louis Nelson," *The Jazz Record*, June, 1946, p. 9.
[17] *A Critic Looks at Jazz*, Jazz Music Books (London, 1946), p. 23.

and Perez all agreed, when questioned independently, that it is hard to say who was "first" or who was "best" but that among the earliest jazz players were: Louis Payton (accordion), Picou, Perez, Nelson, Bolden, and Pete Bocage, who played violin and cornet, was still playing with Big Eye Louis in 1943, and made some recordings that were issued this year in the "Marching Jazz" album on the *Circle* label.

Louis Nelson places most early New Orleans bands a little later than others do. His estimation is as follows: Imperial—1898; Bolden Band (as shown in the *Jazzmen* photo)—1904-05; Superior—1908-09; Eagle —1910-11. These bands were seven-piece groups (most of the time), but did not generally have two cornets, according to the testimony of Nelson and Picou as well as the evidence in *Jazzmen* and other accounts.

While it is not insisted here that the views of the other jazzmen besides Bunk Johnson should be accepted and his rejected out of hand, it is nevertheless clear that some statements that have heretofore been uncritically adopted and spread widely ought at least to be brought into question. It is to be expected that there will be differences of opinion in a field like jazz, where there are so few documents upon which to base historical studies. But where one man's memory becomes another man's article, writers ought to be more careful in offering information to the breathless collectors. Neither the writer's feeling of certainty nor the article's aura of authenticity are sufficient guarantee of the trustworthiness of the claims advanced.

Anyone who has talked with an old jazzman about events long past knows how hazy memories can be and how easily the questioner can draw out answers that he would like to hear, and which are therefore of doubtful accuracy. Because the musician is generally polite and wants to please his admirer, he is apt to agree with the positive statements that are implied in many questions; after all, the jazzman often remembers little and almost invariably cares less.[18] Louis Armstrong, for example,

[18] If a questioner believes that Pops Boldstrong played with King Bechmorton, he can ask King about it in two ways. First, he can say, "King, old Pops Boldstrong played trumpet on a few dates with you at Peachie Black's around 1892, didn't he?" And the chances are that King will say yes. He is less likely to say yes, and more likely to give an accurate answer, if the questioner asks, "King, who played trumpet with you in 1892, at Peachie Black's?" The chances are the King will say he can't remember and will want to let it go at that.

has been quoted as saying that Bunk Johnson was his teacher. Now at one time or another in New Orleans virtually every older player advised a younger one; if that establishes a teacher-pupil relationship, then we ought to start looking for a new word to mean what teacher used to mean. In 1936 Louis' *Swing That Music* appeared. In it he mentions Bolden, Oliver, Louis Nelson, Nick La Rocca, Bechet and Perez—but not Bunk Johnson. Louis also reported in the book that he was influenced by Perez and Oliver, but still no word about Bunk. After Bunk's comeback, however, when he himself had made the claim, some collectors doubtless reminded Louis that the old man had been his teacher.[19]

Some of the pioneer jazz historians and critics are beginning to disparage all jazz writing as superfluous—now that they've gotten in theirs. But if it is important to be told by those who think so that Bunk is the earliest and the greatest living jazzman, then it is equally important for those who have contrary evidence to make their views known too. The origins of jazz and the story of its spread, as well as the careers of its players, are all subjects about which there is still considerable question. The importance of these matters is, in addition, not limited to music itself, or to the interests of collectors or to the reputations of musicians; they are significant, also, for the problems of the origins and diffusion of culture, and racial interaction, which involve other arts as well as some sciences.

The superlative-minded jazz commentators, always pointing out the "best" this or the "first" that, inevitably tend to diminish the stature of other great jazz players, both Negro and white. The jazz community can do with fewer ready-made judgments from oracles about who is the *best* cornetist or the *best* trombonist, or the first collector to hold Bunk's mouthpiece or see his teeth in the glass on the window sill.

[19] It is interesting to note that Preston Jackson, writing in 1935 of the New Orleans days, makes no mention whatsoever of Bunk. (ED.)

I Discovered Jazz in 1902

JELLY ROLL MORTON
from *Downbeat*

A few collectors held on to their Jelly Roll Morton records in the middle Thirties, but it was not until 1938 that he began to be discovered. Early that year Marshall Stearns had written enthusiastically of the great New Orleans pianist-composer, but it was an article in the form of a letter to Ripley, published in the August Downbeat, *which began the process leading to the HRS-sponsored Bluebird dates and the New Orleans Memories album for General Records. This article, a combination attack on W. C. Handy and a puff for himself, was Jelly Roll's bid for fame. It is a complex of history, jazz folk-lore, boasting, and misinformation. It bears reprinting, although not in full, for the picture it gives of Jelly Roll—amusing and pathetic and very human.* (ED.)

IT is evidently known, beyond contradiction, that New Orleans is the cradle of *jazz,* and I, myself, happened to be the creator in the year 1901, many years before the Dixieland Band organized. *Jazz* music is a style, not compositions, any kind of music may be played in *jazz,* if one has the knowledge. The first stomp was written in 1906, namely *King Porter Stomp. Georgia Swing* was the first to be named *swing,* in 1907. *New Orleans Blues* was written in 1905, the same year *Jelly Roll Blues* was mapped out, but not published at that time. New Orleans was the headquarters for the greatest Ragtime musicians on earth. There was more work than musicians, everyone had their individual style. My style seemed to be the attraction. I decided to travel, and tried Mississippi, Alabama, Florida, Tennessee, Kentucky, Illinois, and many other states during 1903-04, and was accepted as sensational. . . .

In 1912 I happened to be in Texas, and one of my fellow musicians brought me a number to play—*Memphis Blues*. The minute I started playing it, I recognized it. I said to James Milles, the one who presented it to me (trombonist, still in Houston, playing with me at the time), "The first strain is a Black Butts strain all dressed up." Butts was a strictly *blues* (or what they call a Boogie Woogie player) with no knowledge of music. I said the second strain was mine. I practically assembled the tune. The last strain was Tony Jackson's strain, Whoa B- Whoa. At that time no one knew the meaning of the word *jazz* or *stomps* but me. This also added a new word to the dictionary, which they gave the wrong definition. The word *blues* was known to everyone. For instance, when I was eight or nine years of age, I heard blues tunes entitled *Alice Fields, Isn't It Hard To Love, Make Me A Palate On The Floor*—the latter which I played myself on the guitar. . . .

I still claim that *jazz* hasn't gotten to its peak as yet. I may be the only perfect specimen today in *jazz* that's living. It may be because of my contributions, that gives me authority to know what is correct or incorrect. I guess I am 100 years ahead of my time. . . . *Jazz* may be transformed to any type of tune, if the transformer has doubt, measure arms with any of my dispensers, on any instrument (of course I'll take the piano). If a contest is necessary, I am ready.

The whole world was ignorant of the fact that *blues* could be played with an orchestra (with the exception of New Orleans). One of my proteges, Freddie Keppard, the Trumpet King of all times, came to Memphis on an excursion from New Orleans. I had him and his band play the *New Orleans Blues,* one of my numbers. *That* was the first time Memphis heard *blues* played by an orchestra. . . .

Happy Galloways played blues when I was a child. Peyton with his accordion orch, Tick Chambers orch, Bob Frank and his piccolo orch. Their main tunes were different pairs of blues. Later Buddy Bolden came along, the first great powerful cornetist. On still or quiet nights while playing Lincoln Park, he could be heard on the outskirts of the City, Carrolton Ave. Section, from 12 to 14 miles away. When he decided to fill the park, that's when he would exert his powerful ability. This man also wrote a *blues* that lived a very long time (thought I heard Buddy Bolden say, ". . . . ., ..., take it away.") This tune was copyrighted by someone else under the name of *St. Louis Tickler,* and published about 1898. Buddy was older than I. I wrote a blues in *1907,* entitled *Alabama Bound.* Someone heard the tune and had it published in New Orleans. . . .

Paul Whiteman claimed to be the King of Jazz for years with no actual knowledge of it. Duke Ellington claimed the title of Jungle Music, which is no more than a flutter tongue on a trumpet or trombone, to any denomination of chord, which was done by Keppard, King Oliver, Buddy Petit and many more, including myself when I played trombone, no doubt before he knew what music was. . . . For many years I was Number One man with the Victor Recording Company. *Tiger Rag* was transformed into *jazz* by me, from an old French Quadrille, that was played in many tempos. I also transformed many light operas such as *Sextet, Melody in F, Humoresque,* etc., and *After the Ball, Back Home in Indiana,* etc., and all standards that I saw fit, more than 35 years ago. . . .

In New Orleans we used a regular combo of violin, guitar, bass violin, clarinet, cornet, trombone, and drums.[1] Freddie Keppard and his band were employed at a dance hall by the name of the Tuxedo. This went badly and he had to cut two men off. Keppard let out violin, guitar and bass and hired Buddie Christian on piano. That was the first formation of the so-called Dixieland combo. William Johnson, Morton's brother-in-law, wanted to come to California with a band. Morton's wife immediately financed the trip. On arriving in Los Angeles, they were hired by Pantages for his circuit, on circuit tour. They came east the latter part of 1914 or early 1915 and invaded New York City. Played at the Palace Theatre for two weeks, breaking all box office records. They were booked by Harry Weber. The personnel of the orchestra was Wm. Johnson, bass; Eddie Vincent, trombone; Freddie Keppard, cornet; George Bakay,[2] clarinet; Gee Gee Williams, guitar; Jimmie Palao, violin; Morgan Prince, comedian. This was the first all-New Orleans orchestra to invade New York. They later joined the show (*Town Topics*) as just another act, and positively stole the show. This was the greatest organization in history until they disbanded. . . .

When I first started going to school, at different times I would visit

[1] Ed Vincent, trombone; George Bacquet, clarinet; D. D. Chandler, drums; James Palao violin; Gigs Williams, guitar; Bill Johnson, bass. (ED.)
[2] Bacquet. (ED.)

some of my relatives per permission, in the Garden district. I used to hear a few of the following blues players, who could play nothing else— Buddie Canter, Josky Adams, Game Kid, Frank Richards, Sam Henry and many more too numerous to mention—what we call "ragmen" in New Orleans. They can take a 10c Xmas horn, take off the wooden mouthpiece, having only metal for mouthpiece, and play more *blues* with that instrument than any trumpeter I had ever met through the country imitating New Orleans trumpeters. . . .

Speaking of jazz music, anytime it is mentioned musicians usually hate to give credit but they will say, "I heard Jelly Roll play it first." I also refer you to Clarence Jones, in the early days around Chicago, and musicians (pianists) like Tony Jackson, Albert Cahill, "Slap Rags" White, Santoy, Blue, Chas. Hill, Black Paderewski, etc. I am sure he remembers when different musicians would say, "there's something peculiar," referring to my playing and arranging, but all who heard me play would immediately become copy-cats, irregardless of what instrument they played. My figurations—well—I guess, were impossible at that time, and arguments would arise, stating that no one could put this idea on a sheet. It really proved to be a fact for years. Even Will Rossiter's crack arranger, Henri Klickman, was baffled, but I myself figured out the peculiar form of mathematics and harmonics that was strange to all the world but me. . . .

My contributions were many: First clown director, with witty sayings and flashily dressed, now called master of ceremonies; first glee club in orchestra; the first washboard was recorded by me; bass fiddle, drums—which was supposed to be impossible to record. I produced the fly swatter (they now call them brushes). Of course many imitators arose after my being fired or quitting. . . . Lord protect us from more Hitlers and Mussolinis. (This letter is signed, "Jelly Roll Morton, *Originator of Jazz and Stomps, Victor Artist, World's Greatest Hot Tune Writer.*")

Jelly Roll Morton on Records

HUGUES PANASSIE
from *Jazz Information*

Jelly Roll Morton claimed he discovered jazz. Hugues Panassié can claim with less fear of contradiction that he founded the jazz Academy. Until the publication in Paris of Le Jazz hot, *material on jazz musicians and the records they made did not exist in any language. The field was chaotic; there had been no attempt to organize the information that floated about among collectors, nor to impose a critical system on the music which had hit certain segments of our musical world with such a profound impact. In his introduction to the American edition published two years after the French edition (M. Witmark, 1936), Panassié stated:*

"My single aim here is to give a precise idea of jazz in its definitive form, to put an end to the deplorable misunderstandings about jazz." He also proposed "to give in a strictly objective way that information which is indispensable for an exact knowledge of real jazz . . ."

In the process of cataloguing the musicians who made jazz, in separating the trends, and in discussing the elements of hot style, Panassié was guilty of many sins, (of errors and misconceptions). But from his pioneering effort stems much of the steady accumulation of information and much of the analysis of today. Panassié was handicapped by his far remove from the American scene and by his utter dependence on phonograph records and the chatter of visiting musicians. It is interesting to note that in Hot Jazz, *the only reference to Jelly Roll Morton is a listing among "other excellent Negro pianists."*

In later years, Panassié made amends for this oversight. The article which follows appeared in the last issue of Jazz Information—*November, 1941. It is not definitive—very little of Panassié is definitive—but in discussing the recorded testament of Jelly Roll Morton, it is a fitting memorial to a great jazz composer, instrumentalist, and personality.* (ED.)

J ELLY ROLL MORTON is one of the great figures of jazz music. It is a joy to see that after having been unjustly forgotten, he has received his proper recognition during the past two years. It is very fortunate, too, that the Victor company has reissued many of Jelly Roll's records; for along with King Oliver's Gennetts and Okehs, Louis Armstrong's old Okehs, and the Jimmie Noone Vocalions, they are the best jazz recordings of the New Orleans small-band type.

Jelly Roll is a first-class composer; besides Duke Ellington I don't know anyone who has written so many charming and attractive tunes. He is also one of the best pianists I have ever heard. People call him "corny" because there are traces of the ragtime era in his music. But this ragtime accent does not prevent him from swinging to the utmost and creating the most colorful and delightful choruses. His touch is extremely sensitive, and reveals a musician full of emotion.

Morton recorded a lot of piano solos, but unfortunately the majority of these is unavailable today. The most beautiful of these recordings is perhaps *The Pearls,* a delightful tune of his own which created a sensation among musicians. Available on Bluebird 10257 are *Fat Frances* and *Pep,* two fine piano solos, much better recorded of course than *The Pearls* and the other older waxings. The music, however, is not as amazing. As for the solos recently issued by General Records, I have not heard them yet.[1]

Let us come now to Jelly Roll's band records. I'll stick to the Victor-Bluebird waxings as they are the best and almost the only available ones.

The first sessions all took place in Chicago, and the band was: George Mitchell, trumpet; Kid Ory, trombone; Omer Simeon, clarinet; Jelly Roll Morton, piano; John St. Cyr, banjo; John Lindsey, string bass; and Andrew Hilaire, drums. Titles were *Black Bottom Stomp* and *The Chant* (BB 10253), *Smoke House Blues* and *Steamboat Stomp* (BB 8372), *Dead Man Blues* and *Sidewalk Blues* (not reissued but should

---

[1] Many of the records cheerily announced as "available" by M. Panassié are unfortunately impossible to get these days. But the General records are still around in some shops and should be on anybody's list. *Mamie's Blues,* in particular, is especially poignant in its evocation of a mood and an era. (ED.)

be, for it features one of George Mitchell's best trumpet solos), *Grandpa's Spells* and *Cannon Ball Blues* (BB 10254), *Doctor Jazz* and *Original Jelly Roll Blues* (BB 10255) and *Someday Sweetheart* (not reissued). A few musicians were added to those mentioned above, for some of these sides; but their participation is rather unimportant.

With the exception of certain parts which are nicely arranged, these records feature mostly solos and improvised ensembles with the classical New Orleans balance between the trumpet, clarinet and trombone. The music, on every side, is almost constantly magnificent. This is not surprising, for all these musicians are first-class players; if I am not mistaken all are from New Orleans, which explains the perfection with which they perform this type of music.

George Mitchell, who deserves much more popularity than he has, is perhaps the most solid New Orleans hot trumpet player, after Louis Armstrong and Tommy Ladnier, among the generation of musicians born around 1900.[2] He sounds very much like Louis and Tommy, and sometimes recalls the sweetness of tone of Joe Smith. Mitchell does marvels with the mute, and nobody should miss his performance in *Cannon Ball Blues,* when he plays the blues with the deepest feeling, or in *Doctor Jazz* and *Original Jelly Roll Blues,* where he plays with terrific attack and swing.

Kid Ory may be considered an old-fashioned musician, but he is my idea of a good ensemble trombone player for this kind of music (just as he was the right man for Louis Armstrong's Hot Five records). As for Omer Simeon, almost everyone agrees that he is a wonderful clarinet player. In ensemble improvisation, he knows perfectly well how to make the clarinet part come out, playing biting high notes which seem to swing the whole band. He is especially exciting in the last choruses of *Cannon Ball Blues* and *Doctor Jazz.* These two sides incidentally are probably my favorites among all those mentioned above.

The rhythm section is worthy of the soloists. John Lindsey plays great bass in all the sides, and John St. Cyr is perfection. I have still to discover a jazz guitarist providing such a beautiful background, for he is just as rich in his harmonies as in the supreme ease of his swing. Listen

[2] In a footnote in *Jazz Information,* Eugene Williams pointed out that George Mitchell was actually not born in New Orleans.

carefully to his part in *Cannon Ball Blues* and *Original Jelly Roll Blues* and tell me if it is possible to play better than he does.

The next sessions also took place in Chicago, in June 1927. The band was: George Mitchell, trumpet; George Bryant, trombone; Johnny Dodds, clarinet; Stomp Evans, alto sax; Jelly Roll Morton, piano; John St. Cyr, guitar; Quinn Wilson, tuba; and Baby Dodds, drums. Titles were: *Beale Street Blues* and *The Pearls* (BB 10252), *Wild Man Blues* and *Jungle Blues* (BB 10256), *Hyena Stomp* and *Billy Goat Stomp* (not reissued but should be, in spite of the "billy goat" effect, for Johnny Dodds' clarinet part is really gorgeous).

These records are quite as good as the former; the same spirit presides over the performances. Mitchell swings powerfully all through *Beale Street Blues,* in which Johnny Dodds takes one of the blues choruses of which he alone has the secret. Baby Dodds' drumming and Quinn Wilson's tuba playing also deserve high praise. The execution of *The Pearls* is beautiful, and an interesting comparison to Jelly Roll's piano solo of the same number. As for Stomp Evans, despite a few bad moments he fits well within the band.

After these records were made, Jelly Roll went from Chicago to New York where all his later sessions took place. The first, in June 1928, almost reached the Chicago standard. The band was: Ward Pinkett, trumpet; Geechy Fields, trombone; Omer Simeon, clarinet; Jelly Roll Morton, piano; Lee Blair, banjo; Bill Benford, tuba; and Tommy Benford, drums. Titles were: *Shoe Shiner's Drag* and *Boogaboo* (BB 7725), *Kansas City Stomps* (BB 7755), and *Georgia Swing* (BB 8515).

Kansas City Stomps undoubtedly is one of the finest of Jelly Roll's records. The tune, typically New Orleans, is taken at a perfect tempo, and Omer Simeon's clarinet is lovely throughout. I should like to draw special attention to Simeon's part in the last ensemble chorus, in which he starts with a grandiose outburst, creating an absolutely exquisite melodic line. It is seldom that such clarinet playing can be heard on records. The tuba work is wonderful too, and I feel inclined to think that few musicians could equal Bill Benford. The rest of the band is good enough. Ward Pinkett, though far from equalling Mitchell, plays the right style.

Georgia Swing features one of Simeon's best clarinet solos in low register, including a few phrases which Teschmaker used from time to time and which he probably borrowed from Simeon.

From this time on, for some reason or other, Jelly Roll did not use such uniformly excellent musicians; and his later sessions are far from as good as all those mentioned above. There were still some excellent players, but others were not good by comparison. Also, some arrangements were used which were not always of the best kind, nor satisfactorily played. So I am not going to say much about these records, except that Albert Nicholas played some pretty clarinet on some of them, *Strokin' Away* for example.[3] One of the sessions (*Mississippi Mildred, Jersey Joe,* etc.) was made with the men from Luis Russell's band: Henry Allen, trumpet; J. C. Higginbotham, trombone; Albert Nicholas, clarinet; Will Johnson, guitar; Pops Foster, string bass; Paul Barbarin, drums; and of course, Jelly Roll on piano instead of Luis Russell. The results could have been excellent. Unfortunately Henry Allen, who plays almost constantly on the four sides, ruins them by a very vulgar, over-exuberant and displeasingly emphatic part. This proves that it may happen that a man born in New Orleans is not for that reason bound to play New Orleans style. These records would have gained 110% if Mitchell had taken Henry Allen's place.

I must also mention the trio records (clarinet, piano and drums) which Jelly Roll made during these years. The first were made in Chicago in 1927 with Johnny and Baby Dodds: *Wolverine Blues* and *Mr. Jelly Lord* (BB 10258). The latter is a delightful tune in the *Baby Won't You Please Come Home* vein, and it features some of the most beautiful piano playing Jelly Roll ever put on wax. Not only are his solos superb, but he contributes a sort of counterpoint to Johnny Dodds' clarinet which is quite phenomenal. Both sides have a very peculiar sound, owing to the fact that Johnny Dodds plays in the low register exclusively.

A single trio side, *Shreveport,* was made in New York in June 1928, with Omer Simeon and Tommy Benford (BB 7710). Simeon, I think, considers it his best record; and certainly it is one of those that really

---

[3] Panassié is only discussing the Bluebird reissues, but it is surprising that he overlooks *Blue Blood Blues,* made at the same date as *Strokin' Away.* In *Blue Blood Blues* (BB 8201), Nicholas plays some of the most exciting clarinet he ever recorded—a solo starting out pensively in chalumeau (low) register, then suddenly stabbing out into high register, and subsiding. (ED.)

do him justice. Here again is a characteristic New Orleans tune featuring a lot of magnificent low-register clarinet, although this time the first chorus and the second part of the last are played in the high register.

In December 1929, the last four trio sides were made: *Smiling The Blues Away* and *Turtle Twist* (BB 10194), *My Little Dixie Home* and *That's Like It Ought To Be* (not yet reissued, though it deserves to be), with Barney Bigard on clarinet and Zutty Singleton on drums. *Turtle Twist* is one of Jelly Roll's loveliest tunes. Barney performs it with the most touching feeling, and Jelly Roll provides a rich and imaginative background. The piano solo, full of melody and nice harmony, is also a gem. In the other three sides, although Barney and Jelly Roll play well enough, Zutty really steals the show with his incredible drumming, alternating terrific breaks on the snare and bass drums with superlative cymbal work. He swings to the utmost when he rolls on the snare drum.

To sum up, Jelly Roll was extremely successful with all his trio records. It is through them that he gave us a large part of his very touching music. And it is not useless to note that he had this trio idea long before Benny Goodman's Trio, which was presented to the public as an innovation, and which always remained far below the Morton trio's performances.

After this period (towards the end of 1930), Jelly Roll stayed away from recordings for about ten years. Only at the end of 1939 did he come back to the studio to make eight sides for the Bluebird label: *High Society* and *I Thought I Heard Buddy Bolden Say* (BB 10434), *Didn't He Ramble* and *Winin' Boy Blues* (10429), *Climax Rag* and *West End Blues* (10442), *Ballin' The Jack* and *Don't You Leave Me Here* (10450). For the first four sides the band was: Sidney De Paris, trumpet; Claude Jones, trombone; Albert Nicholas, clarinet; Sidney Bechet, soprano sax; Happy Cauldwell, tenor sax; Jelly Roll Morton, piano; Lawrence Lucie, guitar; Wellman Braud, bass; and Zutty, drums. For the other four sides the same personnel was used except that Fred Robinson replaced Claude Jones and Bechet was absent.

These are fine records, although not as perfect as Jelly Roll's best efforts. This is partly due to the fact that the band was too big, at least in the first four titles, and partly because some of the men were not at their best, especially Happy Cauldwell. I am convinced that the records would have sounded better without Happy.[4] But Zutty swings wonderfully, Jelly shows by his background work and his solo in *Climax Rag* that he has lost absolutely none of his qualities, and above all, Albert Nicholas plays some fluid and supple clarinet which is a joy to the ear. In *High Society*, when Bechet and he play the celebrated Picou clarinet chorus in turn, he sounds at least as good as Bechet—which means a lot. The best side of the session with Bechet is *Didn't He Ramble*, a lively interpretation which has more drive than the other numbers, and in which Bechet and Zutty especially shine. Sidney De Paris plays well too, but these records don't show him as the great trumpet player he really is.

[4] This is unfair to Happy Cauldwell. The truth of the matter is that no tenor sax could have sounded to advantage in that combination. The alto and tenor just do not fit in with a New Orleans ensemble—perhaps with *any* small improvising group. Somehow, they just don't blend in the tutti, and their solos always seem to hold back the rest of the group. (ED.)

Bechet and Jazz Visit Europe, 1919

ERNST-ALEXANDRE ANSERMET
from *Revue Romande*

*It cannot be too often repeated, to our shame, that Europeans re-
alized the importance and value of jazz many years before the Americans who originated it. Brahms was excited by ragtime, which we
recognize as jazz, in 1898. Ernst-Alexandre Ansermet, the Swiss conductor, was able to make mature and still-valid pronouncements of the
nature of jazz in 1919. His eulogy of Sidney Bechet has long been
famous, but of more significance perhaps is the account he gives us of a
great and forgotten jazz orchestra. His analysis, because it comes from a
trained musical mind, helps us recreate the effect of the Will Marion
Cook band and shows that it was more than less like the real jazz orchestras of today. Ansermet's account, which appeared in the* Revue
Romande *in 1919 was re-published in* Hot Jazz, *the Panassié magazine.
It was translated there by Walter Schaap with whose permission we
present it here. In many ways, it is a documentary, ranking with the
quotations of Frescobaldi's contemporaries in the Roger Pryor Dodge
article.* (ED.)

THIS is not about African Negroes but about those of the Southern
states of the U.S.A., who have created the musical style commonly
known as the rag. Rag music is founded essentially on rhythm and in
particular on the qualities of syncopation in rhythm. Rag music first
came to Europe in the form of the cake-walk, as I recall, and then with
the one-step, two-step, fox-trot, and all the American dances and songs
to which the subtitle of rag-time is applied. America is full of small
instrumental ensembles devoted to rag-time, and if the national music

111

of a people is none other than its popular music, one can say that rag-time has become the true national popular music of America. I remember having travelled by railroad between Berne and Lausanne with a group of young Americans. One of them began to hum a piece of rag-music, whereupon they all joined in, marking the rhythm, by beating their hands on the wooden benches, just as the Swiss in a foreign land, yodel in remembrance of the homeland. Today, rag-time has conquered Europe; we dance to rag-time under the name of jazz in all our cities, and the hundreds of musicians who contribute to our popular music are all applying themselves at this very moment, to adapt this new art to the taste for the insipid and the sentimental, to the coarse and mediocre sensuality of their clientele.[1] Rag-time is even passing into what I will call for lack of another name, the field of learned music: Stravinsky has used it as material for several works, Debussy has already written a cake-walk, and I well believe Ravel will lose no time in giving us a fox-trot. But, under the name of Southern Syncopated Orchestra, there is an ensemble of authentic musicians of Negro race to be heard in London. Instrumentalists and singers, they present us pell-mell with all sorts of manifestations of their art, the old with the new, the best with the worst. It's a mysterious new world which we were acquainted with only through its more or less distant repercussions, and which finally reaches us in its living reality. One can hardly imagine a more opportune manifestation, and it is to be hoped, for our common edification, that the British metropolis will not alone reap its benefits.

The first thing that strikes one about the Southern Syncopated Orchestra is the astonishing perfection, the superb taste, and the fervor of its playing. I couldn't say if these artists make it a duty to be sincere, if they are penetrated by the idea that they have a "mission" to fulfill, if they are convinced of the "nobility" of their task, if they have that holy

---

[1] Permit me another anecdote on this point. One day, while seeking some examples of rag-time at an American publisher's I found one which I rejected because of its dullness and lack of character. Slightly hesitant, the publisher offered me another which he designated as the model of the first; it was a remarkable thing whose accent and force of character seized me at once, but which his clientele would not have, declaring it too trying. The publisher had then made the sugary replica which he had shown me at first, and had withdrawn the original from circulation.

"audacity" and that sacred "valor" which our code of musical morals requires of our European musicians, nor indeed if they are animated by any "idea" whatsoever. But I can see they have a very keen sense of the music they love, and a pleasure in making it which they communicate to the hearer with irresistible force,—a pleasure which pushes them to outdo themselves all the time, to constantly enrich and refine their medium. They play generally without notes, and even when they have some, it only serves to indicate the general line, for there are very few numbers I have heard them execute twice with exactly the same effects. I imagine that, knowing the voice attributed to them in the harmonic ensemble, and conscious of the role their instrument is to play, they can let themselves go, in a certain direction and within certain limits, as their heart desires. They are so entirely possessed by the music they play, that they can't stop themselves from dancing inwardly to it in such a way that their playing is a real show, and when they indulge in one of their favorite effects which is to take up the refrain of a dance in a tempo suddenly twice as slow and with redoubled intensity and figuration, a truly gripping thing takes place, it seems as if a great wind is passing over a forest or as if a door is suddenly opened on a wild orgy.

The musician who directs them and to whom the constitution of the ensemble is due, Mr. Will Marion Cook, is moreover a master in every respect, and there is no orchestra leader I delight as much in seeing conduct. As for the music which makes up their repertory, it is purely vocal, or for one voice, a vocal quartette, or a choir accompanied by instruments, or again purely instrumental; it bears the names of the composers (all unknown by our world) or is simply marked "Traditional." This traditional music is religious in inspiration. It is the index of a whole mode of religion and of a veritable religious art which, by themselves, merit a study. The whole Old Testament is related with a very touching realism and familiarity. There is much about Moses, Gideon, the Jordan, and Pharoah. In an immense unison, the voices intone: "Go down, Moses, way down in Egypt land. Tell old Pharoah: Let my people go." And suddenly, there they are clapping their hands and beating their feet with the joy of a schoolboy told that the teacher is sick: "Good news! Good news! Sweet Chariot's coming."

Or else a singer gets up, "I got a shoes (pronouncing the s to make it sound nice), you got a shoes, all God's children got a shoes. When I get to heaven, gonna put on my shoes, gonna walk all over God's heaven." And the word *heaven* they pronounce in one syllable as *he'm,* which makes a long resonance in their closed mouths, like a gong. Another time, a deep bass points out the empty platform to one of his companions and invites him to come and relate the battle of Jericho, and it's a terrible story which begins, with the mighty deeds of King Joshua and all sorts of menacing fists and martial treads; their hands are raised and then lowered, and the walls come tumbling down. In a lower tone, but with such a tender accent, the quartette also sings "Give me your hand" or sometimes "Brother, give me your hand." There is another very beautiful thing in which a female voice sings the ample sweeping melody (wavering between the major and minor) and of those who are going away towards the valley of the Jordan to cross the river, while the choir scans with an ever more vehement motif, "Nobody was heard praying."

In the non-anonymous works, some are related to a greater or lesser extent to these religiously inspired works, others sing the sweetness of Georgia peaches, the perfume of flowers, country, mammy, or sweetheart; the instrumental works are rags or even European dances. Among the authors, some are Negroes, but these are the exceptions. The others are of European origin, and even when this is not true of the author, it is of the music; most rag-time is founded on well-known motifs or on formuli peculiar to our art,—there is one on the *Wedding March* from *Midsummer Night's Dream,* another on Rachmaninoff's celebrated *Prelude,* another on typical Debussy chords, another simply on the major scale.[2]

The aforementioned traditional music itself has its source, as could doubtless be easily rediscovered, in the songs the Negroes learned from the English missionaries. Thus, all, or nearly all, the music of the

[2] Some time ago, I met in New York, one of the most celebrated rag-time composers, Irving Berlin. A Russian Jew by origin, he had, like Cesar-Napoleon Gaillard, been a jack-of-all-trades, and known all kinds of fortune before becoming rich in writing Negro music. Devoid of any musical culture, incapable of writing his notes, hardly knowing how to play the piano, he told me himself how he used to pick out the notes on the piano with one finger, or whistle to a professional who noted down these melodies which entered his spirit, and how then, he'd have the professional seek out the harmonies until he was satisfied. Having assimilated the Negro style perfectly, it is to this style that he applies his gift of musical invention, which is indeed remarkable.

Southern Syncopated Orchestra is, in origin, foreign to these Negroes. How is this possible? Because it is not the material that makes Negro music, it is the spirit.

The Negro population of North America is African in origin. I am acquainted with the music of the African Negroes. They say it consists in work-songs and ritual dances, that it is based on melodic modes differing from ours, and that it is particularly rich in its rhythm which already practices syncopation. In losing their land, have the Negroes carried off to America lost their songs as well? (One shudders in conjuring up such an image.) At least, they didn't lose the taste for them. In their new villages by the cotton fields, the first music they find is the songs which the missionaries teach them. And immediately, they make it over to suit themselves.[3]

The desire to give certain syllables a particular emphasis or a prolonged resonance, that is to say preoccupations of an expressive order, seem to have determined in Negro singing, their anticipation or delay of a fraction of rhythmic unity. This is the birth of syncopation. All the traditional Negro songs are strewn with syncopes which issue from the voice while the movement of the body marks the regular rhythm. Then, when the Anglo-Saxon ballad or the banal dance forms reach the Dixieland land of the plantations, the Negroes appropriate them in the same fashion, and the rag is born. But it is not enough to say that Negro music consists in the habit of syncopating any musical material whatsoever. We have shown that syncopation itself is but the effect of an expressive need, the manifestation in the field of rhythm of a particular taste, in a word, the genius of the race. This genius demonstrates itself in all the musical elements, it transfigures everything in the music it appropriates. The Negro takes a trombone, and he has a knack of vibrating each note by a continual quivering of the slide, and a sense of glissando, and a taste for muted notes which make it a new instrument; he takes a clarinet or saxophone and he has a way of hitting the notes with a slight *inferior appoggiatura,* he discovers a whole series of effects produced by the lips alone, which make it a new instrument. There is a Negro way of playing the violin, a Negro way of singing. As for our orchestra tympani, needless to say with what alacrity the Negro

[3] It's me, Lord, who needs Thy benediction. It's not my brother, it's not my sister, it's me, Lord.

runs out to greet them, he grasps all the paraphernalia instantaneously including the most excessive refinements, to set up an inexhaustible jugglery.

The banjo itself (string instrument strummed with a pick) is perhaps not the invention of the Negro, but the modification for his use of a type of instrument represented elsewhere by the mandolin.

By the grouping of these chosen instruments, following the most diversified combinations, a more or less definite type of Negro orchestra constituted itself, of which the Southern Syncopated Orchestra is as the first milestone,—an attempt at a synthesis of great style. Composed of two violins, a cello, a saxophone, two basses, two clarinets, a horn, three trumpets, three trombones, drums, two pianos, and a banjo section, it achieves by the manner in which the instruments are played, a strangely fused total sonority, distinctly its own, in which the neutral timbres like that of the piano disappear completely, and which the banjos surround with a halo of perpetual vibration. Now the fusion is such (all brasses muted) that it is difficult to recognize the individual timbres, now a very high clarinet emerges like a bird in flight, or a trombone bursts out brusquely like a foreign body appearing. And the ensemble displays a terrific dynamic range, going from a subtle sonority reminiscent of Ravel's orchestra to a terrifying tumult in which shouts and hand-clapping is mixed.

In the field of melody, although his habituation to our scales has effaced the memory of the African modes, an old instinct pushes the Negro to pursue his pleasure outside the orthodox intervals: he performs thirds which are neither major nor minor and false seconds, and falls often by instinct on the natural harmonic sounds of a given note,— it is here especially that no written music can give the idea of his playing. I have often noticed, for example, that in [their] melodies the A sharp and the B flat, the E and the E flat are not the sounds of our scale. It is only in the field of harmony that the Negro hasn't yet created his own distinct means of expression. But even here, he uses a succession of seventh chords, and ambiguous major-minors with a deftness which many European musicians should envy. But, in general, harmony is perhaps a musical element which appears in the scheme of musical evolution only at a stage which the Negro art has not yet attained.

All the characteristics of this art, in fact, show it to be a perfect ex-

ample of what is called popular art,—an art which is still in its period
of oral tradition. It doesn't matter a whit, after all, whether Negro music
be written by Russian Jews, German Jews, or some corrupted Anglo-
Saxon. It is a fact that the best numbers are those written by the Negroes
themselves. But with these as with the others, the importance of the
writer in the creation of the work is counterbalanced by the action of
tradition, represented by the performer. The work may be written, but
it is not fixed and it finds complete expression only in actual performance.

Nevertheless, some works in the repertory of the Southern Syncopated Orchestra mark the passage from oral tradition to written tradition, or if you choose, from popular art to learned art. First we have a
number for choir, soprano, and orchestra, inspired by the traditional
works, and signed Dett. On a Biblical text, *Listen to the Lambs,* which
Handel too has treated in the *Messiah,* this musician has written a very
simple yet very pure and beautifully enraptured work. Or we have some
works of Mr. Will Marion Cook including a very fine vocal scene entitled *Rainsong.* Perhaps one of these days we shall see the Glinka of
Negro music. But I am inclined to think that the strongest manifestation
of the racial genius lies in the *Blues.*

The blues occurs when the Negro is sad, when he is far from his home,
his mammy, or his sweetheart. Then, he thinks of a motif or a preferred
rhythm, and takes his trombone, or his violin, or his banjo, or his clarinet, or his drum, or else he sings, or simply dances. And on the chosen
motif, he plumbs the depths of his imagination. This makes his sadness
pass away,—it is the Blues.

"These great blue holes which the naughty birds make."

But, for the bitterness of this line, the most refined poet and the Negro
coincide here in their expression.

There is in the Southern Syncopated Orchestra an extraordinary
clarinet virtuoso who is, so it seems, the first of his race to have composed perfectly formed blues on the clarinet. I've heard two of them
which he had elaborated at great length, then played to his companions
so that they are equally admirable for their richness of invention, force
of accent, and daring in novelty and the unexpected. Already, they gave
the idea of a style, and their form was gripping, abrupt, harsh, with a
brusque and pitiless ending like that of Bach's second *Brandenburg Con-*

certo. I wish to set down the name of this artist of genius; as for myself, I shall never forget it—it is Sidney Bechet. When one has tried so often to rediscover in the past one of those figures to whom we owe the advent of our art,—those men of the 17th and 18th centuries, for example, who made expressive works of dance airs, clearing the way for Haydn and Mozart who mark, not the starting point, but the first milestone— what a moving thing it is to meet this very black, fat boy with white teeth and that narrow forehead, who is very glad one likes what he does, but who can say nothing of his art, save that he follows his "own way," and when one thinks that his "own way" is perhaps the highway the whole world will swing along tomorrow.

Louis Armstrong: A Reminiscence

BUD FREEMAN

In the late 1940s, Morroe Berger, who as a professor later brought jazz to Princeton, and I gave a course in jazz appreciation at the Rand School of Social Science. Among those we brought in as "guest lecturers" was Bud Freeman, the very fine tenor saxophone player whose musical history went back to the Chicago days of Louis Armstrong and Bix Beiderbecke. (He was very pleased when we introduced him to the class as "the intellectual of jazz.") In his remarks, Bud discoursed on Louis Armstrong—"the greatest" —who had pioneered in the development of jazz. The following is put together from notes and from memory, and roughly parallels what Bud Freeman said and wrote in later years. (ED.)

I WAS perhaps seventeen when, in 1923, I first heard the great Louis Armstrong play. My good friend Davie Tough, the fine jazz drummer who gave so much swing to the early Tommy Dorsey band, told me about a great band at the Lincoln Gardens, a dance hall in the South Side of Chicago. Davie took me to this place, and through the noise and the smoke I first heard the King Oliver band. We were a couple of white kids, but no one bothered us. And after a few visits the doorman, a very big man, used to look at us as we came in and say, "Well, it looks like the little white boys is here to get their music lessons."

In that King Oliver band, you had Lil Hardin—she later married Louis; Honore Dutrey on trombone; Johnny St. Cyr on banjo—guitar would take over later; Johnny Dodds on clarinet; and his brother, Baby Dodds, on drums. This was the same group that Louis took into the studio when he made his sensational Hot Five records. The Oliver band had a new kind of beat, a real jazz beat instead of the ragtime rinky-dink. They really could swing. The Oliver band would take a stock arrangement and play it from top to bottom (what us jazz

119

intellectuals would call *da capo*) and then play chorus after chorus in which Oliver or Louis or Johnny Dodds took over. They played all the great New Orleans tunes—the tunes Oliver had brought up the river—with Louis on second cornet, that is, playing obbligato to Oliver, and it was unbelievable.

The jazz critics don't give King Oliver much credit these days, but he had a tremendous sense of melody and there were few who could play the blues the way he did. There are some who feel that he didn't let Louis take off enough. But as I remember it, Louis was an important part of the band and he played a real second cornet to Oliver's lead.

I didn't hear Louis playing as a soloist, on his own, until much later at the Sunset Cafe in Chicago. He had gone to New York to play with Fletcher Henderson's orchestra—a band that could really rock or could fall apart, it was so undisciplined, but it created the kind of jazz that Benny Goodman took over and unleashed in the swing era. Benny's first terrific arrangements all came from the Henderson book. In New York, Louis was already a jazz hero because of the Hot Five records he made for Okeh. He was the hick when he hit town—button shoes, cap, you name it. Fletch Henderson was a great bandleader and he had some of the best sidemen with him: Joe Smith, for one, who had the sweetest and hottest tone on horn of anyone this side of Bix. Henderson let Louis take it easy until he was relaxed and then he let him go. From that moment, Louis had the band and Harlem in the palm of his hand, and jazz was never the same.

Take Coleman Hawkins, the tenor sax in the band. He had that big tone, but he was still a little corny until he heard Louis. Louis taught him that beautiful melodic line and that perfect phrasing. Not only the Hawk but almost everyone who was playing jazz in those days was influenced by Louis. You can admire that fluid and stabbing attack of Bix, or Jimmy Noone on clarinet, or any jazzman you can name, and you can see the difference that Louis's way of playing, his whole approach to jazz, made in New York and throughout the country. Even Duke learned from Louis, as he freely admits.

I don't say that Louis invented jazz as we know it. We laughed when Jelly Roll Morton told *Downbeat* that *he* did. Jelly Roll made a very big contribution and so did Sidney Bechet, who was playing in a style twenty years ahead of his time when he recorded with Louis. No one "invented" jazz, but you have to remember that before Louis and

Bechet and Jelly Roll, all we had was a kind of developed ragtime. Even good musicians thought they were doing it when they would take a series of eighth notes and play them dotted. Louis rose above the *da-ta, da-ta* of rag and gave the notes a graceful, limber line—jabbing or *legato*—and a drive that few had.

But Louis left Fletcher and returned to Chicago. He joined the fine Carroll Dickerson band, and Carroll persuaded Earl Hines, playing somewhere else in Chicago, to join the band, not knowing that "Fatha" Hines and Louis would make musical history. There is much talk that Louis changed Earl, who developed "trumpet-style" piano. The fact is that they learned from each other, influenced each other. They were rivals and collaborators, and you can hear it if you listen to *West End Blues* or any of the records they made together for Okeh.

At the Sunset, if I remember correctly, Louis gave up the softer-toned cornet for the more brilliant trumpet. The Sunset had floor shows, and you play a different kind of instrument for a floor show. Louis began to play in the high range, hitting C above high C and high Fs. This was remarkable, but Louis had the lip to do it. There's a story, and a true one, that when Louis gave his first concert at the Salle Pleyel in Paris, he hit a series of high Cs, followed by a high F, and this so surprised the classical musicians in the audience that they dashed onstage to examine his trumpet. They were sure it was specially designed to let Louis play those high notes so easily.

There was another great contribution by Louis—a new way of jazz singing—and this occurred when he returned to New York. I had come from Chicago with Ben Pollack's orchestra, a band that played dance music *and* jazz, with some fine jazz sidemen, and I used to hear Louis at Connie's Inn, the Harlem nightclub. He was not known as a vocalist then, though he had done some singing of Fats Waller tunes. It was in a Broadway musical, *Hot Chocolates,* in which he popularized "Ain't Misbehavin'," that his singing became famous. When Louis sang, he phrased as if he were playing horn, and in that show he developed and popularized what we now call *scat.* Listen to the great vocalists who followed him—Ethel Waters, Billie Holiday, Mildred Bailey, even Bing Crosby—and you will see how much they were influenced by Louis's way of singing, from phrasing to attack to scat, in which you forget the words and hit the notes like an instrument.

In the years that followed, Louis was playing in the top range of the trumpet—not for effect, not to show off as some critics said, but because that was how he felt it and because in that range he was forced to a kind of economy that made his music classical, in the real sense of the word. Mezz Mezzrow says that if you touched Louis when he was playing, you could feel his whole body vibrate. And he gave that jazz feeling to everything he played, even the longhair music.

I sat in with Louis on a number of occasions, and any musician will tell you what excitement it was to play with him. Listen to my early records and you will understand how hard I tried to repeat on the tenor sax his way of playing trumpet. It's easy to say, but perhaps it all began with Louis and it may end with him. And it isn't only that Louis was a musical genius. He was a very special kind of person, a wonderful human being and a man of goodwill. Some people put him down today as an "entertainer"—as if there is something wrong with laughing and joking and reaching out to people. I've always said that Louis had more jazz in him when he told a joke than the rest of us when we're on the bandstand. And there was also sadness in him, as when he recorded *West End Blues* with Earl Hines.

The Wolverines and Bix

GEORGE JOHNSON
from *Swing Music* and *Downbeat*

There was a time when Bix Beiderbecke was called "the greatest of them all"—an exaggeration—and Hoagy Carmichael could be taken seriously when he reported that three notes on Bix's cornet made him swoon. Today, Bix's stock is all the way down and there is hardly a critic who won't go out of his way to take a gratuitous swat at the fallen idol. These swings in popular favor, however understandable, are also regrettable. Bix was a great musician and he did play jazz. As a person he must have been of great personal charm and magnetism. All who knew Bix speak of him with a kind of partisanship and awe which can hardly be musical.

This story by George Johnson, like the Preston Jackson piece, is a documentary—a musician's report of the Wolverines, the band in which Bix began to attract national attention. It is also a record of the conditions under which musicians worked in the jazz era. (ED.)

No story of the Wolverine Orchestra would be complete without at least the mention of the group of musicians, in Chicago, from whom the final personnel of the band was drawn.

This group, with a few whose names have eluded me, played together in combinations of from four to eight or nine as the occasion demanded, for the period of a year or so before the first seven-piece combination, which later was named the Wolverines, started on its first steady engagement at Stockton Club at Stockton, Ohio.

The names of those musicians are as follows: Piano—Dick Voynow. Drums—Vic Moore, Jack Shargel, Bob Conzelman. Saxes and clarinets

—Don Murray, George Johnson, Glenn Scoville, Jimmy Hartwell, Benny Goodman (then in short trousers), Abe (?). Banjo—Bob Gillette, Chuck Cheney, Joe O'Neil. Bass—Ole Vangsness. Cornet—Bix Beiderbecke, Frank Cotterel.

These musicians were the first in Chicago to draw inspiration and gather understanding of "hot music," as played by the "New Orleans Rhythm Kings" at Friars Inn. Every evening found a few of them at Friars, much to that manager's disgust, as they spent little and stayed long. They were there to listen and learn, and to wait long hours until, late at night when the regular members in the band tired, they were permitted to sit in with the orchestra to give a member a few moments' relief. This was a privilege, of course, since the Kings were kings and we all less than that, excepting Bix.

In October 1923, Jimmy Hartwell, who had been playing near Cincinnati, Ohio, succeeded in obtaining a contract for a seven-piece combination to play at the Stockton Club, 17 miles north of Cincinnati. He called Dick Voynow at Chicago and Dick came down with the combination that started on the first extended engagement the orchestra played. That combination was as follows:

Piano—Dick Voynow. Bass—Ole Vangsness. Banjo—Bob Gillette. Clarinet and Alto Sax—Jimmy Hartwell. Tenor Sax—Abe (?). Drums —Bob Conzelman. Cornet—Bix Beiderbecke.

After playing a week or so, the tenor man turned in his notice, and I was called to join the band. I had just returned from playing an engagement in New York with Hoagy Carmichael.

Some time later, in November, Bob Conzelman left for a job in Chicago, and his place in the band was taken by a local drummer named Johnson. This combination continued until the engagement was ended by a riot at the club on New Year's Eve.

The Stockton Club was a type of cafe which could be found in almost any part of the country after the start of prohibition. A large part of the club was devoted to gambling and the rest was a cafe where food and drinks were served and the guests could dance. The club was located on a sparsely populated spot on the road between Hamilton and Cincinnati, Ohio, and was a rendezvous for people from all walks of life, high and low, who enjoyed gambling and dancing until the early hours. The manager, who was as tough a character as I ever hope to meet, was intensely loyal to the band and a great admirer of Bix. He took keen enjoyment in buying drinks for Bix, never ceasing to wonder at the fact that no quantity of alcohol ever made any difference in his playing.

The long playing hours, from 9 p.m. to 4 or 5 a.m., more than any other thing, succeeded in developing that ability of the melody instruments to feel instinctively what the others were going to play next. When the fact is considered that of the recording group, only Voynow and Leibrock could read music, and that each time a number was played, it was played differently except for introductions and passages between choruses, it must be admitted that a complete and perfect knowledge of each other's style was absolutely necessary to prevent discordant harmonic effects and to attain the perfectness of a written orchestration.

To return to the Stockon Club, New Year's Eve found a capacity crowd which, unfortunately, included a part of the gangster element from Hamilton and Cincinnati, two groups between whom existed an intense rivalry and who were separated for the evening, on their promise of "no hostilities," in different rooms. About midnight, two of the party from Hamilton walked through the room occupied by their rivals, took exception to a remark passed, and started what developed into a general riot, open to all. This riot lasted for over an hour during which time the band played *China Boy,* all of us so fascinated by the flying dishes and bottles that no one thought to change the tune. We were told to play, and we played. I have often wished since the day of radio, that we could have broadcast that session. What a record that would have made!

The riot was important to us, aside from its entertainment value, because it meant the end of our engagement there, due to the closing of the club.

We quickly arranged for an engagement at Doyle's Dance Hall, in Cincinnati, to start in two weeks, and all returned to Chicago until that time.

When we returned to start the Cincinnati engagement, Ole Vangsness remained in Chicago to start his dental practice, and we engaged Al Gandee on trombone to replace him, partly because Bix wanted a trombone in the band due to his liking for a Dixieland combination, and partly because no suitable bass player was available.

It was at this time that Vic Moore joined the band and a week or so later, Leibrock, who lived in Hamilton, Ohio, and who had been playing with a theatre band there, came to Doyle's, told us he was at leisure, and was engaged immediately. Min had played with us a few times at the Stockton Club and we were very keen to have him with us. His coming completed the first recording group which made *Jazz Me Blues* and *Fidgety Feet*.

The addition of Moore and Leibrock immediately eliminated a weakness in the rhythm section that had, before their joining, prevented a perfect "oneness" that was so evident in the playing later. Comment has been made by John Goldman in *Swing Music* that much of the swing attained by the orchestra was due to Bob Gillette. That is very true, but Mr. Goldman overlooks, and only naturally so, the drummer, Moore, whose perfect working with the bass and banjo created a powerful, pulsating, steady rhythm that never varied an iota from perfect tempo, and which by virtue of its perfection, allowed the clarinet, cornet and tenor to acquire that ability to play three-part harmony, by ear alone, on even the most difficult figures and passages.

The orchestra would have been lost without that background, and that fact was noted in a small way whenever a strange bass, drummer or banjo would sit in on various occasions. I am very sure that none of the present day drummers, keen though my admiration is of their superb work, could have replaced Moore on a competitive basis if the Wolverines could be assembled today, as they were then. What some do not realize, in listening to old recordings, is that drums did not record in any sense of the word when those records were made and, as a result, the records of the Wolverines give only a half-picture of the true band, with the bed-rock solidity of the drum background entirely missing.

It was during the engagement at Doyle's that we made arrangements to make our first record for Gennett. We left Cincinnati after the job, arrived in Richmond, Indiana, 125 miles distant, at about 3:30 a.m., and spent most of the night wondering how our first "play-back" would sound to us.

No amount of words could adequately describe the excitement and utter amazement of that first recording, played back to us for correction of positions around the recording horns.

Each of us was naturally listening to himself as the sounds came back to us through the horn, sounds that we had never heard before, in so detached and distant a manner. I honestly believe that at that moment, and not at any time before, was born in each of us the idea that as a unit, we had something different in the music line. I doubt if any of us realized until that moment how different in style and how dissimilar in effect our results were from the music of the Friars band that had thrilled us all so, barely months before. Coming to us in that way, out of a horn, the music sounded more like that of another band, and entirely different than it sounded on the job.

I think it will be of interest to mention that we made three masters, at least, of each recording, and if those masters were available today, musicians over the world would have more to enjoy of Bix. We all took different choruses on each master record. In fact, Bix never repeated any chorus he played excepting that he had to learn the chorus he had played on the particular master chosen for printing because people requesting that particular number wanted it played as recorded.

Again, I digress from the story to mention a point concerning Bix, one that I have never seen mentioned before. Although I played with Bix for more than a year and a half, I can honestly say that I have never heard him make a mistake in playing. Knowing his style as thoroughly as we did, we could often detect, in one of his solos, that he had hit a note that he had not intended to hit, but by the time the phrase or passage was complete, he had angled and squirmed out of that difficulty in a run of notes that was so brilliant it would leave us almost breathless. Only his complete mastery, a mastery that was made up of unorthodox fingering, as unique as his ideas, could produce this result. Each chorus of his, every "break," could be depended upon to be new and different. Always exhilarating, his playing was so narcotic in its effect on susceptible listeners that I have seen some that were as truly doped by its effect that they had the manner of an opium addict blissfully happy after his pipe.

Others, like Hoagy Carmichael, in the days when we played at Indiana University dances, would be driven to tantrums of hysteria. We played many a jam session at the fraternity houses at Indiana, with the room packed to twice capacity, and Bix's efforts would produce shouts, the reverberations from which would have crumpled any but a stone house. Surprisingly enough, in spite of all this adoration Bix remained unimpressed, not in the least conscious that the playing he enjoyed so much, was the indication of genius, merely content to play and, of course, tip the cup. I honestly believe he thought all the commotion was homage rendered mostly to the group, when it was more often for him.

Three months passed on the Doyle engagement without incident. We experienced mediocre success, attracting much attention from the musicians in the Cincinnati area but not being a big hit with the majority of the dancers at Doyles.

About the first of April we received a letter from Hoagy Carmichael. Hoagy had met Bix in Chicago over a year previous to this time. He was visiting me and came over to a dance we were playing. He was completely fascinated by Bix's playing and after the job we all went out to the Lincoln Gardens to hear King Oliver and Louis Armstrong, who was playing with King at that time. Later, in January, 1923, Hoagy, Vic Moore and I spent the winter at Palm Beach, Fla., playing private parties and dances, adding local musicians to make 4 to 6-piece combinations. Still later, in the summer of 1923, Hoagy and I played together at a lake resort hotel in New York. During these jobs Hoagy had heard enough about Bix to make him very eager to hear him again.

Our first record intensified this desire, and the letter followed stating that he could guarantee two week-end dances during April, May and June at Indiana University, and at a larger amount of money than we were making at Cincinnati.

We immediately turned in our notice, which our employer would not accept, and we were forced to take "French leave," one of us remaining in the place after closing time and lowering the instruments (which Doyle would not permit us to take out of the building) out the rear window. Cabs to the station and early morning found us in Indianapolis.

Gandee decided to stay in Cincinnati and from this time on we used no trombone in the band.

Charley Davis, whose orchestra was playing at a theatre in Indianapolis, invited us to a midnight jam session at the theatre after closing hours, and at this session, Charley played *Copenhagen* for us. We rehearsed it immediately and it became one of our best numbers and was the next of our recordings.

We played a double orchestra engagement with Charley at the

Indianapolis Athletic Club as our first job in Indiana and realized almost at once from the reception that we were in the right spot.

We were disturbed at first by the fact that for the first hour or so, the crowd gathered immediately in front of the stand, few of them dancing, and only understood the reason when we were told that they were too interested in the style of music to dance. Later, as the rhythm became too intense, they all danced. We were soon engaged for the rest of our time, playing week-ends for Hoagy and the balance of the week at the Casino Gardens night club, in Indianapolis.

At this time Hoagy had the leading dance orchestra at Indiana University and naturally had his own engagements on the same nights as ours. However, he found time to come whenever we were playing, between numbers, and there was always a jam session after the dance at his fraternity house.

During the afternoon of our first engagement there, he played over a song he had written, called *Free Wheeling*. We liked it, rehearsed it and later recorded it under the name *Riverboat Shuffle*. The name was a composite of suggestions from the members in the band, Bix liking the "Riverboat" part and Bob Gillette suggesting the "Shuffle."

That summer was spent in Utopia. Enthusiastic dancers to play to, dancers who understood our music as well as we did, whole days spent playing golf, and a full purse to supply anything we wanted.

Before we left Cincinnati we had all met the cast of the *Abie's Irish Rose* show that was playing in that town. We met nightly at one of the restaurants and with two of the cast in particular, George B. Nolan, who played the part of Abie, and Billy Fay, who played the Irish father, we all planned to play lots of golf when the weather moderated. Fortunately, the show moved to Indianapolis for the summer at the same time we did, and five of us, Bob Gillette, Vic Moore, and I from the band, and Nolan and Fay from the show, engaged rooms at a private home, just a mashie pitch from No. 1 tee at the golf club. All summer we played from never less than 36 to sometimes 72 holes in a day, most of the time under a special ruling allowing a five-some to play.

We lost track of Nolan and Fay after we left Indianapolis in July, and you can imagine my surprise nine years later, while attending a movie, when the familiar face of George B. Nolan appeared on the screen, unexpected, because he had dropped his last name and was now called

George Brent, the latter being his middle name. I often wonder if he enjoys life as much as he used to when he made $150 a week and had nothing to worry about but a nasty slice.

About the 15th of May we returned to Richmond and recorded *Oh Baby, Copenhagen, Susie,* and *Riverboat Shuffle,* using the same combination as before, excepting trombone which we no longer used.

It may be interesting to note that the commercial orchestration of *Copenhagen,* used by orchestras everywhere, was taken note for note as well as could be, from the record we made, chosen before release, as on all other recordings, from the three masters made. Here, more than any other recordings we made, was the vast difference in each of the three masters. If either of the remaining masters has been chosen for pressing, the tune *Copenhagen* as it is known today, would have been very different. This number was made up almost entirely of individual choruses, and we all used different melodies and ideas on the three masters.

Within the next 30 days our records had become generally known, by musicians particularly. Vic Burton, who had just finished playing with a Chicago theatre orchestra, came down to Indianapolis about July 15th with an offer to engage the band, without Moore, for the month of August, to open the new Gary (Ind.) Municipal Dance Pavilion on Lake Michigan.

This offer was a good one and filled in the time until our engagement at Cinderella Ballroom, already booked, to start early in September.

We all decided to take a voluntary cut in salary to keep Moore with the band for that month, and after playing a few vaudeville dates, while Moore took a vacation, we started the Gary job with two drummers. Vic Burton led the band for half of the evening, with Moore playing the drums, and the other half Burton played the drums while Vic Moore rested from the strain of watching a band led by a drummer.

During this five-week period many of our friends from Indiana University who lived nearby, drove over to dance and, as was the custom at that time, each brought a bottle of gin, usually of his own mixing. On one such night I can remember a friend from Indianapolis, crouching behind Bix's chair, holding that worthy's coat collar to the chairback to prevent Bix from taking a tumble. And still the notes rolled out, twice as slippery as ever, due, no doubt, to the lubricating oils in the juniper berries. Those were merry days, with no end of gin to drink, horses to ride, and a grand lake to swim in.

We made no recordings from the time we left Indianapolis until we had been in New York for almost a month, that is, from June until October.

The Gary job ended about the 5th of September, and we all left for New York and the Cinderella engagement.

The Cinderella was one of the finest dance halls in New York, located at 48th and Broadway, in the heart of all that is worth while in the amusement line in that city. Opposite us, playing alternately was Willie Creager's orchestra, the first of four orchestras that played opposite us during the four months we played there.

It was only natural that we in the band looked forward with great pride and no little doubt to our next job at the Cinderella.

Pride, because in less than a year as a definite organization, we were to play in a first-rate spot on Broadway, an achievement rarely attained by any orchestra; doubt, because all our playing had been to audiences decidedly different in the matter of musical appreciation. This, in spite of the fact that Red Nichols, Miff Mole, Jimmy and Tommy Dorsey, Frank Trumbauer and others were playing with different orchestras in the New York district.

There were a few Dixieland combinations in the smaller dance halls and cafes but no combination similar to ours, nor any with a similar style, and for this reason we all looked forward with great anxiety to our opening.

The day before we opened, several of us attended the Hippodrome theatre, where Ray Miller's orchestra was playing a short booking before their opening at the Arcadia Ballroom, just two blocks from the Cinderella.

Miff Mole, Ruby Bloom (whom I had met the year previous in Chicago), and Frank Trumbauer, my personal choice for saxophone royalty, were with Ray. It was our first opportunity to hear them in person. You will understand our enthusiasm when I mention that we all let out a yell that all but drowned out the band when Miff took his first break, and were all summarily ejected from the theatre.

We went around back stage, where I asked for Ruby and where we were introduced to Frank and Miff. The latter was very surprised to learn that we were the cause of all the noise in the theatre. He had thought someone was giving him the bird.

From then on, during our stay in New York, we rarely missed the opportunity of hearing Miller's band on the nights when we started and finished early and they played late, and they came to the Cinderella as frequently.

At that time Ray Miller's orchestra was the first of the large bands to mix a little hot music with the general run of heavy orchestrations, and their hot music would have been a great hit at the present time.

Our contract at the Cinderella was for 30 days, with two options of 90 days and one year. From the very start we were well received, and the word got around Broadway that the Wolverines at the Cinderella were something new and different.

Famous musicians came to listen and were eager to sit in, just as we had been in the days of Friars Inn in Chicago. Most frequent of these was Red Nichols, who at that time was just coming under the influence of Bix's genius. Red probably will not like this statement, but it is my personal opinion that much of Red's playing today is the direct result of the absorption of ideas gained from listening to and playing next to Bix, together with the learning, note for note, of Bix's recordings. Even before we had landed in New York we had heard a recording of Red's called *You'll Never Get to Heaven with Those Eyes,* in which he used Bix's chorus in *Jazz Me Blues* note for note.

Bix was a fountain of ideas that were spontaneous, as unexpected to himself as they were to us, while Red's playing has ever been methodical and carefully thought out, with each note planned ahead. Each was an artist, but Bix had the natural flow of ideas which, once played, were discarded and never used again. There were too many as yet unplayed to bother with repeating.

Our first month was replete with new experiences, being the first trip to New York for any of us. Well received, our option was taken up and we knew we were set until January 1st. We rehearsed new numbers and made our first New York recordings, *Big Boy,* on which Bix played a piano chorus for the first time on record, and *Tia Juana,* about which the less said the better.

Bix spent most of his time after working hours sitting in with some of the Dixieland combinations in town. He always claimed that the five-piece combination was the ideal one.

When we had been in New York a month, Bix gave his notice and joined Frank Trumbauer in St. Louis. I am hazy about this fact, always having believed that he went direct to join Jean Goldkette, but I have since read that he played first with Frank. Our affairs were of primary importance to us and this lack of certainty can be overlooked.

Our first task was to replace him, once he had determined to go. Red Nichols wanted to join us, but we were doubtful, not because of his playing, because we would have been more than pleased to have him, but because of his unreliability at that time. We knew that on his record for the year previous one could never be sure of his being on the job if he happened to feel a bit temperamental. This story might have a different ending if we had.

Paul Mares, in New Orleans, recommended a cornet player there, and we sent him transportation. Mr. Sharky Bonano arrived in all his glory, red underwear and all, played one number, which for his convenience was an old New Orleans song that babies are weaned on in Louisiana, and was given transportation back immediately. I doubt if any man ever made a faster round trip. Nothing but a rubber ball could get to and back as fast as he did, leaving within two hours of his arrival.

A friend of Vic Moore's suggested Jimmy McPartland in Chicago, and Vic called him on the phone. Jimmy at that time could play only in three keys, but in those keys he knew all our recorded numbers, and between many rehearsals and playing with us until Bix left, things went smoothly, with Jimmy fitting right in, shaky at first, but a better substitute for Bix than any other cornetist at that time.

Each orchestra was scheduled to play four numbers as their contribution. We were slated to appear late, about 1 a.m., and were to follow Sam Lanin's orchestra from Roseland ballroom, with whom Red was playing. We planned to play *Copenhagen* and *Riverboat Shuffle,* neither of which had been published as yet, and which, because of our original recording of them, we considered as our exclusive property.

Imagine our surprise when Lanin opened his offering with the one and finished with the other. He had had one of his arrangers sitting at the Cinderella, unknown to us, and had our arrangements almost note for note.

We hastily changed our choice of numbers and played our four, greeted with, as we were told later by N. T. Granlund, the master of ceremonies, the largest reception of any of the orchestras. The dancers, led by the many musicians who had waited since their turn, kept up a steady applause which only abated when N. T. G. promised them that we would play for them again after the remaining bands had appeared. We did play again for several hours and were the only orchestra to play more than our scheduled four numbers.

Our three months' option was taken up and we immediately began to receive offers to leave the Cinderella. Sophie Tucker, Bee Palmer and many others made offers of more money than we were getting.

We were informed by the management of the Cinderella that we were all set for the next year, that our option would be taken up. They also threatened to use legal means to prevent our playing until the end of that year if we left one by one and reorganized, as we considered doing. The result was that we were forced to refuse these offers and in the end were the victims of as neat a double-cross as was ever given anyone.

At about the time we started at the Cinderella, a famous dance team featured at one of the shows in New York a new dance called the Charleston. It is not generally known that this dance started its country-wide popularity at the Cinderella to the music of the Wolverines.

The dancers found our particular rhythm perfectly suited to the Charleston, and the management did everything in its power to forward the popularity, offering prizes for the best team and in many other ways helping to make it the craze it became. For us and the management it finally became the holding of a bear by the tail, lots of fun while you hold, but devilish to let go.

Because of its very characteristics, the Charleston, while a big success, reacted unfavorably to us. Those who did not dance it, and some of those who did, found a crowded floor a disadvantage, objecting to the danger to life and limb in the shape of flying feet, and soon the situation changed; the Charleston dancers came to the Cinderella and the rest of the dancers who liked less violence went elsewhere.

Two months before our three months' option expired no renewal in writing was forthcoming, and we suddenly realized that the assurances given even as late as 24 hours before, that we would be at the Cinderella for the whole of the coming year, were a deliberate double-cross given us because we had thought to leave previously, and due in small part to the uncontrollability of the Charleston situation.

Our offers no longer open, we were out of a job, and suddenly we decided, urged by Vic and myself, to go to Florida for the winter. We left January 3rd and from then on bad luck seemed to dog us. We arrived in Miami, were offered a job almost immediately at a night club, and the night before we were to open, it was closed by padlock by the government for violation of the Prohibition Act.

We played now and then making expenses and enjoying a well-earned holiday. Vic Moore, in the meantime, went to Palm Beach, where his family had been living for three years, and where his father had a very successful real estate business. Vic worked for his father for a few weeks and finally opened an office of his own, made over $100,000 in the next year and lost it one evening when the banks closed overnight with all his cash on deposit.

While in Miami we made arrangements to go back to Indiana for the spring dances, with Dusty Roades as drummer and singer. Advance notices were mailed and we left for Chicago the last of March to replace Jimmy Hartwell, who remained in Miami, and Min Leibrock, who joined Arnold Johnson shortly before we left.

In Chicago we reorganized with Rip Logan, a balmy clarinetist; and a bass player, Morgenthaler, from Min's home town, Hamilton, Ohio.

We played college dances from April 1st until the closing of school, and played other dances on open dates, leaving Thursday, Saturday and Sunday for the Casino Gardens, our old stamping grounds in Indianapolis.

Dissension in the ranks resulted in Dusty leaving, and we returned to Chicago, replacing him with Ralph Snyder, on drums, and using Jimmy Lord on clarinet in the place of Logan, whose balminess became too hard to handle.

We opened at the Montmartre Cafe in Chicago the first of July, played there five weeks and left after experiencing trouble in properly playing the floor show. From the Montmartre we moved immediately to the Valentino Cafe in downtown Chicago, a spot frequented by the underworld element, even as our first job at Stockton Club had been.

This last engagement lasted five weeks, until September 5th, and during this time a rapid series of changes took place in the personnel of the band. Morgenthaler left to start law practice, Bob Gillette left to start in the oil business in Oklahoma, Jim Lindsay on bass and Jimmy McPartland's brother on banjo replacing them.

This left Dick Voynow and myself as the remaining original members of the band, and I think, for each of us, the joy of playing had gone with the many changes. I left shortly after and soon the band broke up completely.

As I think back on those years, the only sad thought is that we allowed the band to pass out as it did, like an old man dying with a weak heart. I'd like to remember that we all disbanded at one time, then I would not have the memory of those last few weeks.

The most enduring memory I have is the pride at having known and played with the greatest artist of all times—Bix the Beiderbecke.

Duke Ellington

WILDER HOBSON
from *Fortune*

*Bands may come and bands may go, but Duke Ellington goes on
forever. The full-bodied music his collection of virtuoso bandsmen dis-
penses may change in color and intent, but it remains the best big band
jazz year after year. And year after year, the jazz critics go to town—
both pro and con—on the Ellington contribution to American music,
to le jazz hot, to whatever particular King Charles's head they subscribe
to at the time. When Benny Goodman was winning popularity polls,
the charge against Ellington was that he did not swing. Today, the
coterie which has surrounded Bunk Johnson and made a cult of that
amazing genius rejects Ellington as "not playing jazz." Despite the
criticism and the acclaim, the Duke continues to turn out respectable
dance music, going his own way as he sees it. And millions of people in
practically every civilized country of the world continue to buy his
records and plug his reputation.*

*In those arid days when comment on jazz in the major magazines was
almost non-existent, every piece that appeared was grabbed up by the
jazz cognoscenti and clutched to the heart. The story of jazz and its
development was still pretty much a closed book and any hints as to
its contents found grateful readers everywhere. When in August of
1933, FORTUNE published a long and sympathetic article on Duke
Ellington and hot jazz, it was an event. For years after, the article was
discussed and avid collectors combed secondhand magazine shops to
get their hands on a copy. Wilder Hobson may not have had all the
answers on jazz then, but in his pioneering he began a trend which has
led to the present painstaking approach which is uncovering the folk*

roots and recording the story of America's most exciting music. Al-
though dated in some respects, the Hobson article is still the best piece
of work on the Duke and merits inclusion in this volume. (ED.)

BEFORE the money changers failed us, it was customary to call this the
Jazz Age. The etymology of the word jazz is obscure. It was once
jass, and some say this was the corrupted nickname of a Negro musician
called Charles. Others think the word has lecherous origins. However
that may be, jazz means different things to different people. To some it
means the whole cocktail-swilling deportment of the post-War era. To
others it suggests loud and rowdy dance music. Many people go so far
as to divide all music into "jazz" or "classical." By classical they mean
any music which sounds reasonably serious, be it *Hearts and Flowers*
or Bach's *B Minor Mass,* while their use of "jazz" includes both Duke
Ellington's Afric brass and Rudy Vallée crooning *I'm A Dreamer,*
Aren't We All?

But Duke Ellington bears just about as much relation to Vallée as the
B Minor Mass to *Hearts and Flowers.* The curly-headed Vallee has made
a fortune dispensing popular ballads to the vast public which always
adores them . . . On the other hand, Mr. Ellington and his orchestra
offer rich, original music, music of pulse and gusto, stemming out of
the lyricism of the Negro and played with great virtuosity. Ellington's
music is jazz; it is the best jazz.

Ellington has just undertaken his first tour of Europe, where he was
resoundingly greeted in Great Britain and France. Said the London
Times: "Mr. Duke Ellington . . . is exceptionally and remarkably ef-
ficient in his own line . . . And the excitement and exacerbation of the
nerves which are caused by the performances of his orchestra are the
more disquieting by reason of his complete control and precision. It is
not an orgy, but a scientific application of measured and dangerous
stimuli." It is no paradox that Ellington should arouse a special personal
interest abroad. He is an idol of the jazz cult which has developed a
critical canon as precise and exacting as that applied to porcelains or
plain song. The jazz cult is apathetic to nine-tenths of modern dance
music—just as apathetic as the old lady who never cared much for the

big bass drum. But the cultist will often go to preposterous lengths to hear or collect records of the remaining tenth, the genuine *hot* music. Furthermore the jazz cult is international. It has no boundaries. In Europe, which is more critical and discriminating about all kinds of music than the U. S., there are many jazz connoisseurs. England and France have magazines strictly devoted to *hot* music. A Belgian lawyer, Robert Goffin, has written the only knowing volume on the subject (*Aux Frontières du Jazz*), which makes such American jazz apologists as Gilbert Seldes and Carl Van Vechten seem positively unlettered.[1] Apropos of Ellington, M. Goffin remarks: "Sans extravagance, avec des moyens tout en douceur et en demi-teintes, Duke a atteint le pinacle de la gloire."

As for the U. S., Duke Ellington and his orchestra have appeared in every large Paramount, Loew's, and Keith theatre in the country; they have played dance engagements from Bowdoin College, Maine, to Frank Sebastian's Cotton Club in Los Angeles; they shared a double bill with Maurice Chevalier in New York and have broadcast innumerable hours over various radio chains; they were featured in Amos 'n' Andy's motion picture *Check and Double Check* and in the late Florenz Ziegfeld's *Show Girl*. All of which means that Ellington is a commercial success. Cleverly managed by Irving Mills, he has grossed as much as $250,000 a year, and the band's price for a week's theatre engagement runs as high as $5,500. These figures are, of course, scarcely to be compared with Rudy Vallée's receipts (with a much smaller band he is estimated to have grossed $312,000 in 1931). But what is remarkable is the fact that Ellington has never compromised with the public taste for watery popular songs, for "show bands" combining music with scenic effects, low comedy, and flag drills. He has played *hot* music, his own music, all the way along: *Lazy Rhapsody* in San Francisco, *Hot and Bothered* in Chicago, and *It Don't Mean a Thing if It Ain't Got That Swing* in New York. Moreover, Ellington himself, a robust, well-poised Negro of Paul Robeson's stripe, is not a showman; he has no such fopperies as Paul Whiteman's three-foot baton and still plays the piano in his orchestra.

[1] This continued to be the case for many years. Until the '40s when Hobson's *American Jazz Music* and the Ramsey *et al Jazzmen* were published and when the HRS *Rag* and *Jazz Information* began to appear, Europe had a monopoly on jazz magazines and serious jazz books. (ED.)

His success with a type of music not noted for its box-office appeal
may be partly attributed to the fact that he is assisted in his theatrical
tours by feature singers such as Ivie Anderson and dancers like the
gelatinous "Snake Hips" Tucker. These performers plus the band constitute the highest grade Negro entertainment, which always has a market of its own. But there can be little doubt that Ellington's success is
mainly due to his music itself. It is the final development of a moving,
spirited, wholly American musical form.

So far as anyone can tell, jazz began with Negroes in the Deep South
circa 1910. It is not very profitable to examine sources—you may easily
be carried back to African rites of spring or plantation songs or, more
exactly, fix on Buddy Bolden, a black cornetist from the Rampart Street
section of New Orleans who played wild notes which never occurred on
his scores and was committed to an asylum before the U. S. entered the
War. For all practical purposes, jazz history begins with black boys of
Bolden's stamp who decorated the one-steps of the pre-War day with
flourishes of their own. With swipes and runs and tantalizing beats
like the patter of a tap dancer's slippers, they took the starch out of
ragtime and injected those sad, unorthodox harmonies which have
echoed for years in the cotton fields.

A cardinal principle of their music was spontaneity. All true jazz
music is built around passages in which the musicians improvise, exercise their personal fancy—and in this lies the difference between true
jazz and ordinary dance music as well as the pretentious concert-hall
syncopation of George Gershwin. Those country fiddling contests in
which rustic Paganinis, inspired by corn whisky, play cadenzas they will
never play again are not unlike the jazz musicians' *jam sessions* where
the players vie with one another in *hot* solos. Jazz classics such as *St.
Louis Blues, Tiger Rag, Royal Garden Blues,* and *Milenberg Joys* are
not set pieces, orchestrated in full. They are merely simple themes en-
couraging ad lib variations by the players. This spontaneity reaches truly
magnificent lengths in the smokiest shrines of jazz, where you will
frequently hear a Negro bandmaster yell "Blues in E Flat!" and launch
out on an excursion all his own, superbly accompanied by men who have
only an instinctive notion where he is going.

Jazz went up the Mississippi via river boat to Chicago (in Memphis,
on its upward journey, W. C. Handy—who still lives in Seventh Avenue

in Manhattan's Harlem—conceived *Memphis Blues* and *St. Louis Blues*). Jazz blared across the West to San Francisco, and was introduced to New York in 1916 at Reisenweber's restaurant by five white ambassadors from New Orleans called the Original Dixieland Jazz Band. They found the town dancing sedately to violins and cellos, and left it jiggling to *Tiger Rag,* composed by the Dixieland's cornetist and leader, D. J. La Rocca. The band made half a dozen Victor records, long since out of print, sometimes earned as much as $1,200 a night, and pioneered jazz for a year and a half in London. None of the boys could read music, all of them were polished players. They made it forever after unthinkable that good jazz musicians could be otherwise. Jazz works on its performers like an intoxicant, and in 1925 La Rocca, fearing a breakdown, shelved his cornet and retired to New Orleans.

He left a host of followers in the field. One impolite dive on Chicago's South Side was featuring the amazingly windy trumpeter, Louis Armstrong, who blew such frenzied tattoos as he has recorded under the titles *Mahogany Hall Stomp, Knee Drops, Skip the Gutter,* and *Muggles.* The Wolverines, a barnstorming white orchestra, featured the late Leon ("Bix") Beiderbecke, a cornetist from Davenport, Iowa. Beiderbecke tempered Louis Armstrong's violence with his own exquisite taste, exhibiting a lyric grace and variety of beat which made him perhaps the most admired white jazz musician. Meanwhile a locomotive fireman from St. Louis named Frank Trumbauer practiced his instrument in his cab and became the favorite saxophonist of the Mississippi belt. In New York, Joe Venuti was playing all four strings of his violin at once, and even this *tour de force* was no more admired than his hot inventions on a single string. In Manhattan, also, Trumpeter Red Nichols gathered a jazz band which devoted itself to hot recordings with all the painstaking care of the Flonzaleys approaching a Mozart quartet.

These men loved their work; when they played for their own pleasure they inevitably played *hot.* There was intense rivalry among them, and a mutual admiration foreign to such egocentric arts as the opera. The jazz musicians gave no grandstand performances; they simply got a great *burn* from playing *in the groove.* But it was only infrequently possible for them to make a steady living with the *hot* style. The public preferred the so-called "symphonic" dance music originated by Paul

Whiteman, who played popular tunes elaborately scored and adorned with snatches of Grieg or Tschaikowsky, and also had great success with dance paraphrases of such standard music as the *Méditation* from *Thaïs* and César Cui's *Orientale*. And so the *hot* men were usually to be found playing for profit under "symphonic" leaders. Sometimes they were allowed to *go to town,* but for the most part they accommodated public taste.

Had jazz not been so staunch, it would surely have received the *coup de grâce* in 1929. That year skirts as well as stocks descended; there was a perceptible revival of gracious manners. The national thirst yearned for something less positive than gin, the tail coat replaced the dinner jacket, and ladies who had sworn never to submit to corsets again were shaping themselves to meet the new order of things. Appropriately, Rudy Vallée breathed a genteel number called *Deep Night* and became almost immediately the highest priced musician this country has ever known. Bing Crosby, who first made a name for himself singing in the jazz style with Whiteman's Rhythm Boys, discovered there was more money to be made with teary effects in the low register and became, via radio, a promising rival for Vallée's popularity. During the last few years there has been less public demand than ever for *hot* music. You hear practically none of it in the leading hotels and night clubs (which do, however, provide much that is *corny*). The radio offers true jazz, along with everything else in the world, but not in conspicuous quantities. It is even losing its great popularity at college promenades. Paradoxically, however, the jazz which persists today is the best jazz ever.

This is explained by the fact that jazz, as has been suggested, has never been dependent on widespread popular favor. It is played because certain men like to play it, and it is played in public because a sufficient number of laymen have always shared the musicians' pleasure. Furthermore, the years have brought the jazz players more and more musical sophistication, more and more technical ability; the jazz spirit is better equipped for expression today than ever before. The best white ensembles usually compromise by playing both *sweet* and *hot* music. This is true of Ben Pollack's excellent *swing* band of Chicago (with Trombonist Teagarden and other crack soloists) and of the superbly drilled Casa Loma orchestra, favorite of Yale promenades and the New England dance-hall circuit, whose Guitarist Gene Gifford has composed and arranged some of the neatest exercises in *stomp* (very fast) time. But since it seems to be congenitally impossible for Negro dance musicians to play *straight,* it is not surprising to find that jazz survives most vigorously today among the race which gave it birth.

Various names are worth mention—Don Redman, Louis Armstrong, Fletcher Henderson, Earl Hines—but it is Duke Ellington, a veritable prince of pulsation, who probably deserves to be called the first figure in jazz today. When Ellington and his orchestra played before Percy Grainger's music classes at New York University, Mr. Grainger drew some casual comparisons with the music of Bach and Delius. "I'll have to find out about this Delius," said Mr. Ellington. The chances are he has never made the investigation. So busy is he with his band and his own musical ideas that he seldom troubles to hear his own phonograph records.

Edward Kennedy ("Duke") Ellington lives in a large Harlem apartment at 381 Edgecombe Avenue—and therefore New York may lay claim to being the jazz capital of the world. Separated from his wife, he makes his home with his parents, a nineteen-year-old sister Ruth, and a fourteen-year-old son Mercer, who prefers drawing to music (even his father's). For many years Duke Ellington's father was a blueprint maker at the Washington, D.C., Navy Yard. Edward Kennedy Ellington was born in the capital in April, 1900. He began studying the piano at the age of eight under a Mr. Grant and a Mrs. Chinkscales. At Armstrong High School he veered away toward painting, etching, and all kinds of athletics, but his mother kept him on the piano stool. At sixteen he began to play raggy music for Washington society with Louis Thomas' orchestra. These were the years when jazz entered the North; the Original Dixieland was enjoying its New York heyday, and in 1918 the late Lieutenant Jim Europe, famous Negro bandmaster of the A. E. F., returned from overseas with a group of black boys who had discovered the New Orleans brand of nerve tonic before the War. One fine day in France, when several bands of the allied nations were assembled in concert, Jim Europe had stopped the show with *St. Louis Blues.* He played it again in Boston a year or so later, and after the performance his drummer stabbed him in the back.

Jim Europe and the Original Dixieland convinced Ellington that jazz

was his medium. In 1923 he toured with one of the earlier and more
raucous jazz bands, directed by Wilbur C. Sweatman, a mammoth
Negro whose specialty was a number in which he found room for three
clarinets in his mouth at once. This feat was not so interesting to Ellington as the pliable idiom of jazz, which barred no experiment and allowed each player to formulate his own rules. The fact that a man could
squeeze a living from such irregular music was almost too good to be
true. Back in Washington a little later, he formed his own band, the
Washingtonians, with Trumpeter Arthur Whetsel, Clarinetist Barney
Bigard, Saxophonist Otto Hardwick, and Drummer Sonny Greer. All
of these men are with him today.[2]

The local success of the Washingtonians encouraged Duke to move
on to New York. He opened at the Kentucky Club in 1926, and was
soon verging on bankruptcy. Almost any New York success requires
press-agentry, and Ellington's jazz had no ballyhoo. Fortunately before
it was too late a press agent appeared. Irving Mills is not a musician himself, but he knows what is distinctive and is an experienced showman.
No one needed to convince him that Ellington was highly potential: he
had heard the band.

The problem was one of sales, and Mills believed that with a larger
orchestra and a distinctive location, Ellington could be made a drawing
card. For a while he flirted with the idea of forming a musical bureau
to be known as the Royal Orchestra—led off by Benny "King" Carter.
Once and for all, therefore, Ellington became "Duke," a *sobriquet* first
earned in his Washington school days. The Royal Orchestras never
materialized, but Mills augmented Ellington's band to twelve pieces,
placed him at the Cotton Club in Harlem (where rents were low), and
installed a Negro floor show, fast, agile, and undressed. A dozen men
were what Ellington needed to give body to his ideas; the radio spread
his name and music throughout the East, and between the floor show
and the band—undeniably the most toe-tickling in the city—the Cotton
Club attracted a large downtown clientele. Ellington had arrived.

Ellington composes perhaps half the music his orchestra plays, and
stamps his personality unmistakably on the rest. In addition to those
already mentioned, among his best numbers are *Mood Indigo, The*

[2] As of 1947, only Hardwick and Greer remain. Whetsel is dead and Bigard is out of the
band. (ED.)

Mystery Song, The Dicty Glide, It's Glory (Victor), and *Blue Tune, Lightnin',* and *Ducky-Wucky* (Brunswick). His best recorded versions of other music include *Limehouse Blues* and *Three Little Words* (Victor), and *Rose Room, The Sheik,* and *Blackbirds Medley* (Brunswick). Ellington uses fourteen men—three trumpets, three trombones, four saxophones (doubling on all manner of reeds), piano, guitar, string bass, and drums. Very frequently the sections are employed in unison, the six-part brass team playing in counterpoint against the four reeds with the remaining players acting as percussion. But Ellington has no set rules of orchestration. His conceptions are miniatures; and in the titivating mysteries of rhythm, tone color, and interweaving voices, Ellington is an adept. R. D. Darrell, writing in the magazine *Disques* declares: "To me . . . the most daring experiments of the modernists rarely approach the imaginative originality, mated to pure musicianship, of a dozen arresting moments in Ellington's works."

While Ellington's music is personal and finished to the *n*th degree, there are always *hot* solos by the players—the jazz fundamental is preserved. Ellington's instrument is not so much subservient to him as sympathetic. The understanding between the men is uncanny: Ellington and his drummer, Sonny Greer, for instance, engage in a constant signaling with eyebrows, hands, or grimaces. It is no exaggeration to say that his band of fourteen can *fake* (improvise) as adroitly as the early five-piece combinations. Usually the music is a striking blend of arrangement and invention, typical of which is a trumpet player stabbing bright patterns through lustrous curtains of tone.

Ellington hates the spade work of writing music. At rehearsals, which are frequently called for three o'clock in the morning, after the night's work is done, no scores are visible. The leader seats himself at the piano and runs over the theme he wishes to develop, shows the men what he thinks the saxophones might play here and the brasses there. Perhaps Barney Bigard, the solo clarinetist, suggests a rolling phrase on the reeds at a certain point; it is tried and judged by general opinion. Freddy Jenkins, the electric little trumpeter, may favor muting the brass in various passages. Each man has his say. After four to five hours of this informal process, a new number has been perfected—suavely and intricately arranged, played with the utmost technical command. Ellington believes his men memorize more easily this way than they would by using prepared scores. Most of his famous arrangements have never been written down; sometimes, after five or six months, Manager Mills succeeds in persuading Ellington to put one on paper. The *hot* solo passages are, of course, left blank, with some such notation as *"get off."*

But there is really very little reason why Ellington should bother to score his arrangements. They are so difficult that few other dance bands can play them at all, and very few with anything approaching the ease and spirit of Ellington's musicians. Reading his scores, other orchestras quickly discover that he continually expects things from his men which even the best players elsewhere are seldom called upon to deliver. He conceives his music, for instance, in terms of piano chords and indicates certain notes for the fourth saxophone, regardless of whether the intervals and sequences are convenient for a saxophonist to play. Ellington knows his men can play them; other leaders are not so fortunate. Manager Mills wastes considerable money buying Ellington special arrangements of standard tunes. By the time the orchestra plays them they are Ellingtonian—lustered with his own harmonies, pungent with his rhythm.

Ellington spends his spare moments writing a score for a Negro musical show to be produced next season by John Henry Hammond Jr., son of the New York lawyer, and one of the leading jazz connoisseurs of the country.[3] Ellington is also conceiving a suite in five parts, tentatively titled *Africa, The Slave Ship, The Plantation, Harlem*—the last being a climactic restatement of themes. Whether this will be arranged for his band as now constituted or for an augmented group has not been decided. The composer expects to leave the piano, taking a baton in the form of a drumstick which, while conducting, he will beat on an elaborate choir of tom-toms. And he is trying desperately to find a reed instrument lower even than a contrabassoon with which to produce voodoo accents in the opening section. His friends say he will ultimately invent one. With this suite in his repertoire, Ellington may some day make his Carnegie Hall debut.

It will be an occasion—but, depend on it, there will be no concert-hall piety about the affair. Harlem offers a foretaste of it this very day. In Harlem hot music survives. In Harlem argument survives—the jazz

[3] Needless to say, this show has never been written. Ellington and Hammond have fallen out—for musical and other reasons. (Ed.)

boys debate the merits of two Negro pianists, the partially blind Art Tatum and Willie Smith, somewhat terrifyingly known as The Lion. And in Harlem Duke Ellington and his men have a traditional place in the purple glow lamps of the Cotton Club. Presiding high above his fellows is the dapper Sonny Greer, surrounded like an alchemist with his tom-tom crucibles and tympanic retorts. In the delicacy and pertinence with which he approaches these instruments he is the very symbol of elegant, seething syncopation. There, while Ellington's brass sprays out the steaming measures of *Ring Dem Bells* and Greer titillates the chimes, listeners may remember their Aldous Huxley and cry out: "What songs! What gongs! . . . What blasts of Bantu melody!"

Benny Goodman and the Swing Period

FRANK NORRIS
from the *Saturday Evening Post*

Swing was more a sociological phenomenon than a musical expres-
sion. The reviews of the critics after Benny Goodman's first Carnegie
Hall concert, and their disappointment at the sounds they heard, demon-
strate this point. Swing hit the country as it pushed out of the depression
doldrums. Musically it was a dilution of jazz, but it helped to re-awaken
interest in the real thing. For this, we must all be grateful. Moreover,
swing was played by jazz musicians who found a way to compromise
between their music and the commercial product. The excitement which
hit the jazz world when the swing craze broke upon the world is proof
enough that swing had something very real to offer.

If any one name is associated with the swing boom, that name is
Benny Goodman. For it was his band, playing Henderson arrangements
and utilizing the driving power and inspiration of jazz, which led the
invasion against the sickly-sweet strains of the Lombardo-Vallée schools.
Goodman was the first real rags-to-riches success in the swing-jazz field
and his story, told by Frank Norris, one of the Life-Time *jazz clique,*
is almost in the Alger tradition. But packed away, too, is a considerable
helping of jazz lore. (ED.)

WHEN Benny Goodman opened at the Paramount in New York
last winter, six or seven hundred people had already been waiting
outside an hour when the sun came up. At six o'clock there were 3000
of them, mostly high-school kids from the Bronx and Brooklyn and
Staten Island. Squeezing themselves in their windbreakers and leather
jackets, they began to dance and shout and light fires in the gutters along

Broadway to keep out the sting of a January morning. At 7:30 the West 47th Street precinct police station ordered Sergeant Harry Moore to saddle up and proceed with ten mounted men to the scene, and as he did so his tolerant Celtic intelligence must have dwelt on the ways of the world and the variety of a policeman's experience. This was the first time the sergeant had ever been sent on a riot call at daybreak to herd a crowd of children in to hear a jazz band play.

On the sergeant's advice, the management opened the theater at eight o'clock, for by this time Mr. Goodman's fans were multiplying by the minute, pouring up out of the Times Square subway exits like bees from a smoked hive. Fifty-five ushers, called for special duty, marshaled 3634 of them inside before the fire department ordered the doors closed. The police detail was also increased and went into action on two fronts: Outside, where about 2000 disappointed youngsters were massed out into the streets, paralyzing early-morning traffic; and inside, where the luckier music lovers were stampeding around the lobbies and aisles. Never before in the city's history had police been called for duty *inside* a theater. But the cops had not seen anything yet.

On the screen, Mae West absorbed a number of gentlemen in high collars, but the audience viewed the proceedings with great restlessness, unbroken until Miss West ululated her final line, a rosy light prophetically suffused the orchestra pit and the sound of a wailing clarinet was heard. The orchestra began to rise on its elevator platform, revealing first the brass section, Jess Stacy at his piano and Harry Goodman slapping his bass. Then, below them, Gene Krupa behind his alabaster drums, two rows of teeth flashing as they champed gum in four-four time. Then the reed section and—yes, the clarinet, the glittering spectacles, the smiling, Punch-like face of the veritable Goodman. Out in front, it sounded as though Navy had just completed a long forward pass for a touchdown.

Radio people claim that three nights a week 2,000,000 people are listening to Benny Goodman broadcast. If you ever heard him, chances are you would not forget him. His chief characteristics are definition and power, the rhythm instruments—piano, drums, bass—sound and sure, solidly thumping out the time, while the melody, carried by the concerted brasses and reeds, pulses just a fraction ahead to give the urgent off-beat, the brasses a fine strong burr and the reeds swirling

with improvisations on the tune. And then Goodman's clarinet, clear
and unhurried and artful, playing a song that was never written and
may never be heard again. No other band of this quality has ever had
such popular acceptance. In the past year and a half it has sold more
records, played longer runs and scored higher radio ratings than any
band of its kind in the history of American popular music. When you
hear it play over the radio, you want to beat your feet. When you hear
it play in a dance hall or hotel ballroom, you want to dance. In an audi-
torium, the audience reaction is almost pure violence.

Unhandicapped by either weight or age, the Paramount audience
began clawing at the chairs before the band got through its first chorus
of *Satan Takes a Holiday*. Gene Krupa's drums got off to an orgiastic
uproar on the second chorus and certain shouts from the crowd became
shrilly intelligible: "Feed it to me, Gene! Send me down!" Goodman
took a chorus. "Get off, Benny! Swing it!" And then, trampling ushers,
the children began to dance in the aisles. There were policemen in front
of the bandstand, but some of the kids got by them and up on the
stage. They did the Shag, the Lindy Hop, The Big Apple—all the
leaping Harlem dances—while Goodman grinned and dodged them.
This went on for a solid hour.

In fact, with interludes of Mae West, it went on six times a day for
three weeks. It cost only a quarter to get in for the morning show, so
that was the one the kids mainly came to. But the platoon of experts
who soon arrived on the scene to explain the phenomenon and put it
down to juvenile hysteria overlooked the fact that when the old folks
trooped in to the night performances, they raised Ned, too. Unlearned
in the Big Apple, they tried to express their unity with the ceremony
by clapping their hands and beating their feet in cadence. That, too,
would begin with *Satan Takes a Holiday* and end with the long
crashing finale—the "Killer-Diller," as Goodman calls any cumulative
superlative—of the antiphonal *Sing, Sing, Sing!*

By the time the engagement was over, Goodman had smashed everyone's previous attendance records—including one of his own the year
before—the director of the New York School of Music prepared a bill
for the legislature making swing music illegal, and a New York University psychologist turned the light of pure science on the audience
reaction. "It's simply that a combination of circumstances has made them

one-minded and their inhibitory checks have broken down," he explained. "Some individuals are more suggestible than others, and those individuals start them piling into the aisles. They do sound like goats, don't they?" Other observers were reminded of a camp meeting, the crusades and the thirteenth-century dance madness.

And in the meantime, American popular music had reached and passed an important milestone. In its ups and downs, jazz had had plenty of devotion. But no other jazz band which had conscientiously and uncompromisingly stuck to playing the real stuff—supposedly unsalable to the public—had ever achieved such extraordinary popular reception.

Benny Goodman is a national, not a New York phenomenon. The autograph hunters, those telltale scavengers of the successful, keep him on the run in Los Angeles, Chicago, Detroit. In Philadelphia, not long ago, a strange mishap befell two Goodman fans. Waiting outside the theater all night in order to be among the first seated in the morning, they went to sleep standing up. An alarm clock in one of their pockets was set to arouse them at six A. M. When it went off, it spooked them so badly that they fell through a plate-glass window. The man who causes all this excitement is a highly talented, very effective and richly likable bundle of contradictions just past his twenty-eighth birthday. That makes him and jazz about the same age. In fact, they grew up together.

The Dixieland Jazz Band was just coming in off the street and looking around for a piano player who couldn't read music when Benny Goodman squealed his first note in the Chicago ghetto. The Dixieland had gone to Chicago, to New York, to London, had put jazz in the language and a fortune in its pockets. And now, with Art Hickman and the first wave of big sweet bands calling the country's dance tunes, the Dixieland was on its last vaudeville tour when Benny's father heard that they were giving away musical instruments over at the synagogue. They were also giving away music lessons, so Father Goodman took Benny and two of his older brothers, Fred and Harry, to see what was going on. He figured they might want to make their living that way. Benny's father was a garment worker, but he hoped the boys would not have to spend their lives in a clothing loft. It wasn't a bad idea at all. With varying success, all the boys turned out to be musicians. Fred became the trumpet player on the old Ted Lewis band. He is now doing something else, having gone out with the high C. But when middle G was good enough for the customers, Fred was a pretty fair trumpet player. Harry took up the bass fiddle. He now plays it in Benny's band. And if Mr. Goodman were still alive, he would no doubt be glad to know that Benny, who chose the clarinet, paid income tax on $125,000 last year.

The instruments were lined up around the wall in the synagogue basement, and Benny picked the clarinet because, with all its shiny nickel keys, it looked the prettiest.

In return for their lessons and the instruments, the boys were expected to play in the synagogue band. Benny, however, promptly made the first of the many shifts that were to take him and his clarinet all over the country. He left the synagogue and joined the Hull House outfit, for what inducement he no longer remembers.

When Benny was eleven, he was sent to a German music teacher named Franz Schepp. Notwithstanding the fact that he charged the Goodmans only a dollar a lesson—if it had been any more there wouldn't have been any lessons—Schepp was a rather famous Chicago musician. A number of members of the Chicago Symphony had studied under him, and Goodman recalls this opportunity with gratitude. "He taught me how to use the instrument right at the right time." Benny was eleven. This exposure to the classical tradition is just now beginning to take full effect, with the result that, while Goodman plays the music of each well enough to excite critics of serious music, he frankly states that whereas Mozart is a cat, for him Brahms is not in the groove.

But in 1921 Benny was not under the influence of dead Germans but live American Negroes. King Oliver had come up from New Orleans several years before—the general migration of American syncopation was up the Mississippi and turn right—and his protégé, Louis Armstrong, had his name in lights out in front of the Black Belt's famous Plantation. These two colored trumpeters strongly influenced all the musicians who listened to them. And Benny listened to them all he could. Chicago was a great place for a hot musician to grow up in in the early 20's. It still is, but perhaps the giants seemed to be a little bigger then. Jimmy Dorsey had come out west from Scranton. Out of Davenport there was Bix Beiderbecke, whose improvisations on the trumpet were often pure lyric poetry. He was not only interested in the colored men but hung around the College Inn a lot, listening to Tony Panico. The town was full of young ride musicians, and some a little older, who were showing them which way to go. Jazz music, in spite of the big, sweet, suffusing movie-house bands, was on its way to its second pinnacle.

Benny Goodman's first professional engagement was at the Central Park Theater on the far South Side. His act was an imitation of Ted Lewis. Ted got him the job. That summer Benny and some other kids began playing for dances at Electric Park in Waukegan, Goodman filling the engagement in short pants. He was still in short pants the following summer when the band got a job playing on a lake boat that left the Navy Pier at lunchtime and returned from Michigan City, across the horizon in Indiana, after supper.

To date, most Goodman biographies have been as riddled with small confusions as Mahomet's. Goodman himself often stops, when coaxed into an autobiographical conversation, to say, "Now let me see. Now wait a minute. Oh, *yeah*——" The middle 20's are particularly turgid. When talking about this period, he chiefly recalls that "things got to going sort of fast in here."

But there are scenes that stick, like sitting in his bedroom at home, with the elevated clanging by outside and the door shutting off the rest of the family, the right foot beating the time, the clarinet crying the different ways in which *Japanese Sandman,* or *Rose of the Rio Grande,* or *No, No, Nora*—pop tunes of the day—were not written. His heart lifted up with the clearly reached high C, and it was good to feel the sure, increasing nimbleness of the fingers on a run of double notes. Then there is the scene of Bix coming down to the boat—he had worked on it the summer before—and, seeing Benny on the orchestra stand, telling the pudgy kid to keep away from the instruments. And then there was putting on long pants and joining Ben Pollack's orchestra, because by then they were already comparing Benny to Frankie Teschmaker and Milt Mesirow and Peewee Russell. Jazz has its prodigies too. Benny was fifteen.

There is a picture of him, a fat boy of seventeen or eighteen, with the band outside the M-G-M Studios in California. That was the summer that Pollack played a dance hall in Venice; and in the long afternoons, in the cheap seaside hotel where they lived, Benny and Glenn Miller and the boys would sit in a bedroom and talk music and listen to Bix on the records, or the Cotton Pickers, or even old Dixieland records, for Benny liked, above anything else, the rich but inornate style of Rapollo.

Things got going even faster after that. Back to Chicago, on to New York at the Little Club, where the ginger-ale bottles wore bibs saying you mustn't pour them into gin. And there were the Princeton house parties and a long date on the Park Central roof, during which he doubled in the pit band of Hello, Daddy, and somebody downstairs in the hotel shot Mr. Rothstein.

In the Dixieland era and just after the war it was called jazz. Scott Fitzgerald used the word to describe an age. In the feverish late 20's it was hot music that Pollack's and Don Voorhees' and Goldkette's and Red Nichols' bands were playing. Now they call it swing, but it's the same kind of music.

To come to the quick of the whole simple business, you begin with the fox trot. It took a lot of music to make the fox trot—spirituals, blues, ragtime, barbershop quartets, the breakdowns of the barn dances. Broadly, the result was a song thirty-two bars long in syncopated four-four time, with one strain stated and repeated, a variation in the middle and then back to the first strain. This is America's native music. It is history's most highly developed popular music, superseding the Viennese waltz, and wherever western culture has penetrated, the fox trot is the music people dance to. Again talking elementals, there are two ways to play a fox trot—as it is written, and as it is not written. The process of playing it as it is not written is, basically, jazz. True jazz is the product of a creative imagination; the musician taking the melody, exploring it and presenting it in one or many new and different ways. The fox trot has been developed and improved most in the peak periods of jazz playing, when pure jazz was being played and accepted most widely. For jazz is experimental. It is constantly trying for new and freer uses of its instruments, and the impromptu melody that a hot player blows one year is the written music of the next.

The fox trot got its first impetus in the Dixieland period; it slid along rather unexcitingly during the succeeding era, when it was being played straight by the big sweet bands. It got another push in the late 20's—in the popular imagination, Paul Whiteman was the musical cairn that marked and symbolized this elevation. Then it coasted down the slope of depression and began to mount to its present high about the time of repeal. It is worth noting that each of these three peaks coincides with an advance in the technology of distributing music. The Dixieland became a national institution because of the phonograph. Electrical recording was simultaneous with the boom jazz peak and the radio has now put swing, or something that passes for it, in everybody's parlor. But in the last analysis, the men who play jazz make its eras, and if any one musician brought about the Swing Age, it is Benny Goodman.

Those last months before the crash were as mad and merry to Goodman as anybody else. He was making records with different outfits, playing in shows and going out to Astoria to record for the new talking pictures, as well as doing his stuff every night at the Park Central. He was taking in $300 a week from his work, and something on the side from the hot and reliable tips on the stock market that a Middle Western banker's daughter used to come up and give the boys in the band. But the stock market was pretty remote to him, and he remembers the dread winter of 1929 chiefly as the period at which he quit Pollack and joined the pit orchestra at the big new Paramount Theater. Nine years later his name was outside on top of the marquee.

But winter finally did overtake the cricket. After playing in the pit of two Gershwin shows, Strike Up the Band and Girl Crazy, Goodman decided it was time he had his own show band. He organized one and put it in something called Free for All, which, when it reached Broadway, lasted about as long as a bicycle race. And here Mr. Goodman's biography enters a long and unhappy period of what he calls "scuffling." These were very dark days for jazz as well as Benny Goodman. Armstrong had gone to France, most of the other hot men had given up, turned utterly and dismally commercial or taken refuge from the depression in the house bands of radio stations. Goodman ducked into a radio station, too, but he didn't stay there. He knew the kind of music he wanted to play, and if he couldn't play it in a ballroom, he'd play it in a recording chamber. So, in the winter of 1934, he got some of the boys together and made a remarkable series of disks—*Texas Tea Party, Down Home Rag, Dr. Heckle and Mr. Jibe,* and a dozen others. A steadfast and indissoluble body of hot fans, who had just about decided that jazz had gone to join the passenger pigeon, sent up a shout of thanksgiving when it heard these historic records. And just about this time liquor came back and Billy Rose came into Goodman's life. Rose was turning a dark theater into a cabaret, and Goodman got a chance to organize his second band to play in it.

Perhaps the two most pronounced Southern accents in New York belong to Heywood Broun, who was born and raised in Brooklyn, and Benny Goodman, who was born and raised in Chicago. Nobody has ever explained Broun's, but Goodman got his because he has spent a good part of his life with colored musicians. His present band is all white, but two Negroes, the vibraphonist, Lionel Hampton, and the pianist, Teddy Wilson, join him and his drummer in playing hot classics during intermissions. And although he does not employ them, Goodman enthusiastically admits that the drummer, bass player, trumpet player and tenor and alto saxophonists that he likes best in the business are all black. So what he wanted when he signed up with Billy Rose was an organization like Fletcher Henderson's old band, only white. His instrumentation was that of the big Negro bands—five brass pieces, four reeds, four rhythm—and he bought orchestrations from Benny Carter and Edgar Sampson—later Jimmy Mundy and Henderson himself—all Negroes.

When his engagement was over at Rose's Music Hall, it looked as though a period of scuffling was in sight again. But Goodman was due for a little piece of luck at this point and he got it. Some radio people heard the band its last night at the Music Hall, and it was hired for twenty-six weeks to play with two other bands on a three-hour Saturday night commercial broadcast. People began to talk about Benny Goodman's music—particularly young people. To keep the band swinging right, his managers—he had got a firm of these by now—sent him around playing one-night stands at dance halls and parties in the East. According to The Promhawk of Holy Cross College, Goodman's band made the 1936 Junior prom there "far more than a dance ordinaire." And the American Business Survey, noting with surprising timeliness and acumen that Goodman's band was now the favorite of young America, declared: "He's restored the torrid type of rhythm to the position it held before the days of Lombardo."

But while Goodman's public was wildly enthusiastic, it was unprofitably small. When the boys played their first movie-house date, in Pittsburgh, no riot squad was necessary. The theater's box office registered a new low gross for the week. When they opened at the Roosevelt Grill in New York—the cradle of Lombardo—a palmist billed as "Miss Julienne of Hollywood" read Goodman's hand and guardedly ventured: "Benny is a born specialist. It happens to be music, but it might have been science." Luckily for her professional reputation, Miss Julienne made no optimistic predictions as to the length of Benny's engagement at the Roosevelt. It lasted two weeks. The next stop was Elitch's Gardens in Denver. The band had a contract for the summer season, but the manager volunteered to buy it up the third night. The music was too loud, the beat was too deep, it was all too disturbing. You had to listen to it. Some more scuffling seemed in the offing, but there was never any quit in Goodman. He stuck to his style—fourteen men in the groove, the heritage of all that was best in American rhythm music. In fact, the few weak pop arrangements he had acquired he threw out. And that was what saved him. People might not like him—they might never like him—but they didn't forget him in a hurry. He might be disturbing, but he wasn't commonplace. He was powerful stuff—in fact, a killer diller.

The great break, the 1000-to-1, almost unattainable thing musicians and show people spend their sleepless nights dreaming about, came late that summer in Los Angeles at the big Palomar Ballroom. The first night was a great success—friends and musicians and movie people all over the place. The second and third and fourth nights were all right too. Then came the uneasy time. "We were waiting," says Goodman, "for our loyal fans not to have any more money." But apparently they never ran out. He made the Palomar a place for big bands to play, and when he came back a year later, it was at triple the price.

The Congress in Chicago had the reputation of being the graveyard of dance bands. Goodman went there to play six weeks, played there seven months. The town's night life had not had such a lift since Oscar Wilde showed up down the way at the Palmer House in satin knee britches. The Chicago Rhythm Club—part of the new United Hot Clubs of America—put on Goodman Sunday concerts that you couldn't squeeze into with a shoehorn. Marshall Field's named a dress after him, a cigarette sponsored him on the air, and when they made a movie in which Leopold Stokowski was faded out as Goodman's band came on playing *Tiger Rag,* there was not much doubt that Benny Goodman was in.

Goodman's picture has been published so often that he can no longer avoid attracting a crowd if he wears the familiar spectacles and podium grin. That way he looks like an amiable assistant professor of chemistry at some large city college. But if he takes off the glasses, puts his hat on the middle of his head and assumes a long face, the transformation is fairly staggering. He looks like a solemn high-school senior and no autograph hound ever spots him. He is in New York about half the time, and five of his nine brothers and sisters live with him and his mother. He works long hours—rehearsals, auditions, just seeing a lot of people about things—and doesn't get home much except to sleep. The man whose band plays some of the most explosive music ever heard is bothered by noise and has to have a silencing ventilator in his bedroom. But Goodman takes pretty good care of himself. He plays a good deal of tennis, in Hollywood with Groucho Marx. After a broadcast or a stage show, he is usually sweating like a horse, and like a horse he gives himself time to cool out before doing something else. Work takes a lot out of him.

In jazz it's the fans that invent and use most of the really extraordinary slang. Most of the musicians talk pretty straight, and if you were to ask Goodman to go whacky on the gobble-pipe because there were a lot of alligators out front, he might understand, but would scarcely approve. When he expresses himself in musicians' argot, he either does it because it amuses him or because he thinks it's expected of him—and he always says it with a smile. People who know him well think he is about as good company as there is, but he is not the running gag that most hot musicians are supposed to be—and a few, like Jimmy Dorsey, are. However, Goodman is not incapable of cracking fairly monumentally wise, as witness the occasion on which he described the music of a rather whiny trombonist as sounding "like a Chinaman trying to tell you something."

The band took in $350,000 last year all told, and of that about a third went to Goodman. A third went to the players, and expenses and commissions took up the rest. Most of the players get about $10,000 a year. A few, like Krupa—who just left the band to form one of his own and is replaced by Goodman's old schoolmate Dave Tuff—make as much as $15,000. There doesn't seem to be much Goodman likes to spend money on, however, except clothes. He goes to one of the best American tailors in New York, but very probably only someone who goes there too would notice it. He doesn't bother with non-essentials. In the synagogue back in Chicago he found the thing that is valuable to him—music. At the end of a day during which he has played five shows and rehearsed in between, he is likely to go up to Harlem, join Count Basie and some of the boys, and jam old favorites for forty minutes at a stretch. That is the way a jazz musician has fun.

The fact of the matter, of course, is that as a jazz instrumentalist Goodman was about as good the afternoon Bix told him to keep away from the instruments as he is today. And the music his band plays—although it has probably evoked a more eager response than was ever before given a musical organization of any kind—is even better than most of its auditors know. The common mass reaction to Goodman's band is instinctive. Audiences start cheering for a passage before it is completed. They have even been heard applauding an instrumentalist before he starts doing his stuff—and the accolade could not have been one of recognition, because the man had joined the band only that morning.

Perhaps the best way to find out the band's real excellence is to listen to the product of some of its contemporaries. The stolen figures, meaningless ornamentation and poverty-stricken imagery of second-rate tune salesmen—not that Goodman cannot sell a tune—makes out an impressive case for the Goodman band.

The question that seems to agitate everybody who knows Goodman —except Goodman—is how long it will all last. As to Goodman as a clarinetist, there isn't much question. On the authority of Mr. Leopold Stokowski, there are very few people who can play the clarinet as well as Goodman. As to his band, the chances seem to be that Goodman will have quit playing straight dance music long before people will have had a chance to get tired of him.

Just before he went to the Paramount last winter he gave a concert in Carnegie Hall, a place which, for an American, commonly lies behind the seventh veil of a musical career. Variety reported the occasion under the head: GOODMAN'S VIPERS SLAY THE CATS, BUT SALON CRIX DON'T SAVVY JIVE. Which meant to say that Goodman's players—here is a small

horse on knowing Variety, for a "viper" is a marijuana smoker—had
pleased the fans—another on Variety; "cats" are players—but classical
critics had not been able to understand improvisation. The critic whose
failure to savvy was most pronounced was the man from *The Times,* who
said he did not hear a single original figure played, and thus, understand-
ably, got tired of listening to the same tempo for two hours. His reaction,
however, was not the same as that of a number of classical musicians
present, among them the celebrated concert violinist, Szigeti. To them
there was a great deal of the melancholy of Delius in the massed saxophone choruses of *Sometimes I'm Happy.* In the last few minutes of
Sing, Sing, Sing, Stacy's piano hesitantly came through the reced-
ing brasses and played three intricately beautiful variations on the
melody. Then Stacy and Goodman delicately explored it together and
Goodman ran up to the top note and held it as the piano faded, a long
hopeful note that made you think inevitably of Strauss and Zarathustra.

"That was C above high C," said Szigeti afterward. "It's impossible.
How did you do it?"

Goodman grinned. "It was an accident."

A few nights later Goodman sat in with the Coolidge Quartet from
the Library of Congress and they played Mozart's Quintet in A Major
on his cigarette broadcast, over several account executives' dead bodies.
It was quite a popular success and encouraged Goodman in a new notion
which is still in the hope stage. He would like to play nothing but concerts. Thanks to his tenacity and the radio, he has given hundreds of
thousands of people their first taste of honest, uncompromising hot
music. He would like to find a way of going on and giving them something more serious. It is a strange—or at least unexpected—ambition for
a twenty-eight-year-old jazz clarinetist, but he is in earnest about it.

He is of the school which plays Mozart *vibrato,* with feeling, and he
thinks there is as much room for variation and creative interpretation
in chamber music as there is in *Riverboat shuffle.* Indeed, he finds most
chamber music played in a way that sounds cold and unfeeling to him.
To him classical music is hospitable and sympathetic, and he would like
to make it so for masses of people.

He puts a famous Hungarian recording of the Quintet on his phonograph. "See? See what I mean?" An expression of great distress comes
from behind the glasses. "These guys don't know what it's *about.*"

Then he puts his own recording on. The clarinet speaks to the piano, accepts part of the piano's statement, but goes on to develop a point of its own. Goodman listens and smiles. "I wonder what Mozart and some of those other guys would think of this?" he asks, a little wistful—and very sure.

Piano in the Band

OTIS FERGUSON

from *The New Republic*

In the early days of the "swing" flare-up, most of the day-to-day enthusiastic writing on jazz was being done in the colleges. Robert Paul
Smith, then an undergraduate at Columbia, was reporting the news of
Harlem and its music in Spectator and Review as early as 1933. In the
following years Eugene Williams and this writer were trading information with other college critics and arguing with the present co-editor of
Metronome that Clyde McCoy's Sugar Blues was not the world's greatest record. What you could read in the general circulation magazines on
jazz was usually inaccurate, full of phony razz-ma-tazz, or else pain-
fully limited.

It was not until '36–'37 that hard-hitting, excited, yet sound criticism
began to appear, written in an infectious style that carried the author's
enthusiasm. Vehicle for this criticism was The New Republic, and the
writer was Otis Ferguson. As a chronicler of the sights and sounds of
that hectic era in jazz history, Ferguson focussed attention on a number
of musicians whose fame had not penetrated beyond the small group of
"collectors" and aficionados, and the lustiness of his approach lent a
heroic touch to a school of writing which had swung chaotically from
pedantic to jitter-buggerish.

Otis Ferguson is dead today, a name on the long list of men who died
to keep our sea lanes open in the black days of the Nazi submarine war.
Of the handful of articles he wrote on jazz, the incisive profile of Jess
Stacy (published in the New Republic of November 24, 1937) is the best
and belongs in any significant collection of critical reportage of a passing day. (Ed.)

THEY buried Bessie Smith just the other day. She was a great handsome chunk of a woman and still so much in her prime you'd never dream her fifty years; but they picked her out of an automobile smash-up in Memphis and put her in the ground, and now there is nothing left of Bessie, who was the great girl they called the Empress of the Blues. And so I think it is a good idea to speak about the good musicians who are left, as quickly as we can, while they are still among us.

When you go to hear the great Benny Goodman band in New York (the word is great; and you'd better go), you will notice after a time that the band has someone it uses for playing the piano. This piano player will never steal the spotlight. He is slight, youngish, but with a shot of gray in his absolutely straight black hair, and with a sort of funny Irish face, usually absorbed. He is getting a permanent hook in his back from reading scores off a flat piano top (he knows most of them by heart; just studies them to pass the time now), and his natural attitude is one of a kid doing algebra homework, dutiful and patient but cribbing the answers—he snickers to himself, for example, when he finds a little hole Benny hasn't plugged up and drives a minor third into it. He is a Chicago musician, from the old-time big-time; his name is Jess Stacy.

If you move up closer you will hear him come in for a little digging now and then, Gene Krupa giving him that extra *bum bum* on the foot pedal, "Hey Jess," and Benny raising his eyebrows in the signal for what-the-hell-goes-on-here, or coming over to buzz a couple of high clarinet tones right in Jess's ear, and Harry looking down from the bass like the full moon. Jess proves to be just the butt for that sort of thing, because his face begins to get red and flustered, he ducks his head a little lower, which makes his eyes bug a little as he tries to keep everybody in sight and the score too, and he twitches as though one of the girls had tickled him in a severely unmentionable place just as the curtain was going up (Aw, *fellers,* cut it out will you?), and you can see his hands begin to hop. But if you are that close, you can hear how that big band piano is getting played.

Jess Stacy is above everything else a band pianist, the hands powerful on the full heavy chords, the fingers trained down to steel in bringing out both ends of an octave at once through any din, wrists, hands and fingers quick and skimming in a working musician's economy of motion. In such a job, some play a style that is clearly expressed in the term "ump-ah," and some in the butterfly style—*i.e.*, you don't do much until the orchestra pauses for breath, when you immediately play a little right-hand fiddle-dee-diddle of notes above the staff, spattering the place with Duchin, in brief.

Jess plays neither style or all of them, for he uses the piano as both an orchestra in miniature and a linking force among its separate parts, tying the chorded beat of the rhythm section into the melodic line, providing a sort of common base as between brass and reeds, filling out the chords of each. His own summing up of it has the true clarity of one who must find words for his meaning, not a meaning for his words: "What I try to do—" Jess says. "Look, I try to *melt* with the band." It is a simple word, but all the meanings are there in it: nuance, mood, touch, attack, phrasing, harmonic direction, what not. Because it is still in the unspoiled charm of its youth, this jazz music has never troubled to build a complicated breastwork of definitions. Jess and the rest have an *active* knowledge of how a tune may run, of how the value of a chord may be shifted—by its place in the general pattern (where it rises from and leads to), by its attack, duration, the color of its key and measure of its contrast, the sonority dependent on which of its notes are uppermost.

All these things are in his ears and head and fingertips, that is what he's up to as he sits on the bench there, with his head craned over and his hands hopping, his ear sharpened for all the voicing of instruments, building up under the soloists or falling away to quiet backgrounds, letting a good chord bang out against the beat. Unless you sit under the piano you might not notice him at all in his general place, because he does not shoot cuffs or shake his hair down, and never bounces up off the keyboard as though it were a balloon tire and caught him by surprise. But then the band comes down to the release and Benny holds up one finger and Jess nods. Yes, he'll take it; someone floods the spot over, the faces on the floor turn, and 1, 2, 3, 4—1, 2 . . . *Jess!* And there is Jess out in the open all by himself. At which time he seems to draw into the piano, very small behind its bulk and in all that light, and his hands begin to fly both ways from the center—and you'd think he'd been waiting all his life to catch a piano and this one was going to fade away in another minute. On a quiet night you will be close enough to watch his face, as red and foolish as ever and a little more, because the lines around his mouth twitch and his long nose gets a sort of wrinkle, and he takes on the silliest look as he sneaks up on some special close harmony and holds off everything else to make it ring like a gong, and then pretends to play off away from it, and then pounces back onto it, driving it in cross-rhythms three, four, five times over.

If you listen with some love of the stuff you will hear many things in the spare phrasing and calculated attack of this music. There are echoes from way back, and there is a special background in music—the attitude toward it and way of playing it developed by the boys around Chicago years ago, when jazz was coming up the Mississippi from New Orleans and shifting its center to Chicago. Krupa is from that center, Benny and Harry Goodman are too; but Jess Stacy is a man who goes back farther, older than any of them though still in his creative youth. He goes back to James P. Johnson and Pine Top Smith, beyond the time Louis Armstrong left the riverboats to work in Chicago and New York. And you can hear not only the new beauty of each figure as he plays it, but the overtones of the tradition it is played in, what he gathered from the best men and now plays in memory of their genius.

Jess Stacy was born (1904) in Cape Girardeau, Missouri, a town 150 miles down the river from St. Louis. He started on piano when he was twelve. His family being respectable Irish and poor, he went to high school and scrabbled around at odd jobs between times—jerking sodas, playing small non-union dates, at one time working as a hand in a barrel factory. He got to within a few credits of graduation and then went on working. Finally, at the age of twenty, he got his first really professional job, $35 a week and room and board, with the band on a riverboat.

The boats came into town with as much gala as possible, inviting passengers to go aboard for an evening of dancing on the river, to the strains of their absolutely superior dance orchestra. (Jess got $5 extra a week for playing the calliope as the boat came in around the bend); up and down the river and all its navigable tributaries, from town to town, for thousands of miles. He covered the whole network before he was through. All the time he was hearing musicians; long before, he had gone to hear Fate Marable's band when it played his home town, with Louis Armstrong riding his silver horn, with Babe and Johnny Dodds; and that was the time when *Whispering* came out. And after a while he noticed, when they played a certain town, a little old round-faced kid who came aboard nightly to listen, his eyes wide and cheeks still like an apple—a shorty kid who'd never more than heard of a bottle then, but had such music in his heart that in the brief years before the bottle got him he released some of the finest notes in the country—Jess saw Bix Beiderbecke and sat in with him later, and still in 1937 speaks his name with reverence and happy memory, for he will endure no other trumpet player before him. Bix sat in with Charlie Evans in Moline, Illinois, and later played the Greystone Ballroom in Detroit with Jean Goldkette; and at that time his peer, Louis, was at the Sunset Cafe in Chicago.

Jess kept playing and listening, getting nowhere much himself but going as high as $95 a week in Chicago music. Then the down grade ("bye and bye hard times"), and all the miserable salary cuts, lack of notice. He actually got down as low as $21 at the Subway Cafe when John Hammond came across him there. He had lost all hope, with all his friends dead or forgetfully famous, playing his fine music as un-compromisingly then as he always had—but who was there to hear it, outside of the night's handful of stumblebums? He got back up to $55 by the time Hammond got onto Goodman, and Goodman got an open-ing, and gave Jess the call.

About any musician who has to pull it out of himself as he goes along, the same thing is true as of poets: there are stretches of stuff that any competent man could have done, and then, the burst of something that till now was never done, never imagined, lovely with the dew on it. On the latest Hampton record of *After You've Gone,* for example, Stacy's solo is good average piano for the first six bars—and then there is this thing the boys mean when they say "out of this world," running strong through four bars, gradually tapering off through the last ten. Analyzed, it is simply the old piano blues style (a sort of *oink*-ily, *oink*-ily, *oink*-ily effect), but it comes in at just the spot in just the register to mix pleased recognition with delighted surprise, banking two separate phrases against each other to link them inextricably. With his Quartet, incidentally, Teddy Wilson does the same sort of thing in a double-faced record called *In a Mood,* a blues. In this case it is a man carrying forty-eight bars that are beautiful throughout, but rising even above that in his sixth and seventh. Both of them, one Negro and one white, are playing the same instrument at the top of their field, working in the same organization. Otherwise they are two different men. Wilson is more creative and his own melodist; Stacy is more the man who swings the band, always listening.

Jess Stacy has had those comical ears of his spread for music so long that it is a pleasure and a means of correction to go over musicians with him. "He doesn't make it sing like Bix," I say; and "You know a thing about Bix? He didn't give a *damn*," Jess says; and we each know what the other is talking about.

And when Teddy is playing between sets or with the quartet, Jess has his ear turned sideways and his mind remote from the chatter around the table. He once copied off a Wilson solo broadcast from the playback note for note ("to see if I could just find what makes that man so *good*"). I'm not talking about surface poses, arms over shoulders for the camera, etc.; I mean from long hard day to long hard day. "Anybody I *really* admire," Jess is liable to blurt out any time of the night and off the record, "it's that little old Wilson." It is rather funny to see them independently, both quiet at their work, the younger man (Jess was learning the trade when Teddy was three) getting all the limelight of the quartet work and gathering fame about him like heat lightning, the veteran playing longer hours for less attention, and none of this rushing to the head or bile of either. Presently the band is up and Teddy comes to sit behind Jess's piano, to watch his hands. "Only wish I could work up a hand like that," Teddy says, spreading his fingers out in a full octave chord on the table to illustrate reach and power, nodding in Jess's rhythm with a sort of admiring regret. It is funny to see them, but there is also something restful, unique and sweet about this open honor for another man's worth. It is common only to the best artists and even among these (take a look around, just take a look around you), it seems to open out most easily in those arts, no matter how ragamuffin on the surface, that are nearest to the best in life, living their work without any fuss.

From the deep background of the blues and from his own feeling, mind and hand, Jess made twelve bars of piano on a record that John Hammond supervised for English Parlophone, *The Blues of Israel*. That one is a sport all through, but after a few playings the piano stands out as much as anything. It has so completely that old-time pensive mood in the treble, the slurred second and the close three-finger chord hanging a mood of nostalgia around such a simple progression as sol, fa, mi, re; it is given so thorough a support in the constant working bass, whose left hand mingles intimately with what the right is doing. The song hangs on a trill, doubles the time for a swinging phrase, and slows to an ending of sustained chords, beautifully voiced. The analysis is simple, but the effect runs over into those complexities of the musical spirit that cannot be rightly described—and so it may be wiser just to say what the boys would say, speaking out like an infield: "*Play* that piano there, you Jess. It sure is pretty."

He is a great fellow for the blues, but in his fourteen working years, up and down the country, in and out of pavilions and barrel houses, he has taken all the styles discovered into his own style: the complex running bass of Pine Top Smith's boogie-woogie, a sort of reverse boogie-woogie he remembers from Lucky Roberts, way back; the Earl Hines and James P. Johnson of the old days; some single-note trumpet phrases from Bix and Louis; forgotten derivations from some chance genius of the honky-tonks—above all the free, steady drive of the drums-guitar-bass part of a band (no good rhythm man may follow the beat, but must lead it, have the swing in him to carry it and the iron to hold it against gathering tension and fatigue).

So he runs from *The Blues of Israel* to the terrific and back-breaking tempo that Gene Krupa and a bunch of madmen held on the Victor recording of *Swing Is Here*. He runs from the sophistication of a solo on Benny Goodman's *Madhouse* to the jazzy Dixieland blare of the *Maple Leaf Rag* (Paul Mares and his Friars' Society Orchestra). About the best of all is the way he used to eat up the choruses on *Sing, Sing, Sing*, getting higher with each one and beyond himself, truly wonderful piano. (Benny, like the swell musician he is, would stand beaming and silent through all of them, but when they recorded it somebody was wrong, because there is everything on the double-side twelve-inch release except that perishable triumph.) The first time I heard it was at the New York Paramount, and when I began cheering afterwards backstage, all Jess would say was "Oh, you mean that old A-minor-chord thing; it's all right, that chord." And much later they were playing some sad backwater where the bloods were yelling for

Casa Loma Stomp and failed to get the idea of a solo and bawled for brass. And Jess dug in and took about five in a row, so mad they couldn't get him out of it, and it was beautiful—they didn't want to take him out. All he said after that was, "I'll teach them what to holler for, the icky bastards." (*You know a thing about Bix? He didn't give a damn.*)

But those are the recordings, the outstanding flash parts; and Jess Stacy more than almost any musician of his rank has little to show there. The deep consistent music of his piano still comes out best only to those who play over it or sit there under its sounding board. About which words lead only to more words—so go to hear him in town, or when the band plays a one-night stand in some town near. And when he plays, you listen; and when he possibly comes over to your table afterwards and talks, you listen; and when he says, Let's sneak out and get a blast out of that jug the man has over at the bar, you go along. You will for once be near the singing tradition of this country and its people, nearer than you know.

Grandfather of Hot Piano

BY ROSS RUSSELL
from *Jazz Information*

*The jitterbugs don't line up when James P. Johnson begins to play.
He is perhaps a jazz musician's jazz musician. He is also what Charles
Edward Smith called a "key man in Harlem piano,"—an elaborate but
poetically true pun. For many lovers of jazz, James P. is the greatest of
the living jazz pianists as well as a creative musician of the first order.
Unlike Jelly Roll Morton, James P. is a modest man, which may account
for his relative obscurity.*

*The facts of James P. Johnson's life are here told by Ross Russell, in
an article reprinted from the November, 1941,* Jazz Information. *But it
gives only a small idea of the genius and productivity of an outstanding
maker of music. He has left many records in his wake, but most of them
are hard to get these days and give but a small notion of his contribution
to the store of jazz.* (ED.)

JAMES P. JOHNSON, often called the "grandfather of hot piano," is a dis-
couraging subject for a biographer, which may explain why he has
been overlooked so often by critics and historians of jazz. *Jazzmen*
failed to mention James P. once in its three hundred odd pages; and this
could hardly have been the intent of the editors of that excellent book,
but rather the difficulty of tying him in with the tradition. Unfortunately
Johnson never rode a coal cart in his life. He never played piano in a
whore house, got expelled from Austin High, experimented with cigar-
box guitars, purloined a beat-up trumpet from a pawn shop, or even
fiddled with the instruments on a riverboat. The facts are definitely
against him.

Johnson was born and grew up in New Brunswick, New Jersey, and that is a far cry from Storyville. For his first instrument he had to go no farther than the parlor of his own home, and for a first teacher, his mother. He came by his music and his medium of expressing this music logically, naturally, almost casually. That he achieved his success with a minimum of frustration and deviation is perhaps a tribute to his innate genius; and the fact is yet more amazing when we see that his creative talents were constantly being threatened with complete obscurity by a tremendously active and successful career in the field of Negro commercial music.

He was born February 1, 1891, a contemporary of the New Orleans giants who were to fashion the first principles of jazz just after the turn of the century. His mother, a fair amateur musician, taught him to play a rag on the parlor upright as soon as he was old enough to manipulate the keys. When that had been committed to memory she taught him another, and after that stomps, more rags, and a few blues. At the age of nine James P. was apprenticed to a local piano teacher for regular lessons. Here Johnson got a real break. The teacher, one Bruto Giannini, was an old country musician, a strict disciplinarian, a man of scales and exercise books. Somehow this Giannini possessed the good judgment not to meddle with his new pupil's natural bent. James P. was allowed to play his rags and stomps, but with an important innovation—only after the fingering had been corrected.

Looking back, Johnson is happy about this strange apprenticeship with the old-school maestro who helped him give form to the still crude material. Along with correct fingering, Giannini taught the boy harmony; enough at least to augment a splendid natural ear and unlock the technical mysteries which popular music might hold. So equipped, James P., just entering his teens, took the cold plunge into the sea of professional music that was then beginning to lap at the shores of Manhattan.

His first full-time job was that of "piano kid" at Barron Wilkins' cabaret in New York. Here he played the popular stuff of the day, seasoned with liberal doses of ragtime. Here he met and became intimate with one Charles "Lucky" Roberts. Roberts, a whimsical maniac, had a considerable reputation as an entertainer and "eccentric pianist."

Roberts' influence made itself felt during Johnson's formative period, leaving its deepest impression in the brilliant right hand which marks

the grandfather's style even now. But this was mere keyboard showman-
ship, a fact which Johnson recognized and wished to remedy. He wanted
a solider, more two-fisted style than Roberts' and, gigging around the
big town, he found his answer in the work of one Ablaba, a bordello
"professor" who, according to James P., had a left hand like a "walking
beam." This was the inspiration for James P.'s walking bass.

During the teen years Johnson worked steadily at various bright spots,
satisfying the patrons, and at his own style, expanding and tightening
it so that by the time of the great jazz boom he was able to emerge a
full-fledged virtuoso. Immediately following the epoch-making Reisenweber stand of the Original Dixieland Jazz Band, Johnson took advantage of the boom. With Shrimp Jones, Nelson Kincaid, Ford Dab-
ney and others, he formed a band and bid successfully on the Clef Club
job. This combination, fronted by and featuring Johnson at the keyboard, made a long stand at the Clef and helped establish the reputations
of most of the men in it.

When the date finally expired, and the musicians drifted away to
organize bands of their own, Johnson decided to explore a fresh medium,
that of vaudeville. Here he found himself in competition with a popular feature of the four-a-day circuit in Professor Benjamin Harney, billed
as the "Outstanding Exponent of Ragtime Piano." Johnson accepted
the challenge and after a single season had overhauled Harney in popularity. He played the circuit for several years, finding time meanwhile to
launch hit tunes of his own composition such as *Mama's and Papa's
Blues* and the still durable *Stop It, Joe.*

Swinging back to New York City and the Palace just after the Armi-
stice, Johnson heard of a new field, one which was soon to feel the full
force of his talents. Colored musical comedies, tailored for roadshow
consumption, were usurping the place of minstrel companies. Johnson talked his way into the musical directorship of an elaborate production to be known as *Dudley's Smart Set.* After writing many of the
lyrics and rehearsing the numbers, Johnson went on successful tour
with the show, covering much of the South and West. 1920 found him
back in New York again.

James Reese Europe had just returned from the Continent and was
reorganizing the old Hell Fighter band for domestic exploitation.
Europe asked Johnson to take over the piano. This offer, combined with

his own urge to play live music once more, was too much for James P. to ignore. He accepted, and the Europe band went into the Clef Club for a long engagement. During this period James P. made his first player piano rolls for Ampico and Aeolian. In 1921 he was approached by the larger QRS company and signed to make rolls exclusively for them, as a "race" feature alongside the rococo but immensely popular efforts of Phil Ohman and Zez Confrey.

So far Johnson had never waxed a phonograph record. But this was soon to come, for the phonograph companies had tapped a field larger than that reached by the piano rolls. Once the Original Dixieland Jazz Band platters had tested public receptivity, Confrey and Johnson were won away from the QRS concern. Victor soon advertised solos by each in its ever-expanding catalog. Jimmy's first Victor pressing was *Bleeding Hearted Blues*. The popularity of this record, probably the first (jazz) piano solo on wax, is attested by other releases which followed in 1922 and succeeding years on Okeh, Columbia, Brunswick, Black Swan, and other competing labels.

Important as these items are to discographers, they were merely side-lines with James P. Now he can scarcely remember how many sides he made, or when; he is frequently confronted with something he knocked off one afternoon in a recording studio and has never heard since. When Alfred Lion and I talked to him at his home in Jamaica, Long Island, he had completely forgotten about *Harlem Strut,* for instance, and was still anxious to acquire copies of the far commoner Brunswicks.

At that time record dates were merely a useful source of side money, just like song royalties. In fact, James P. was better known as the composer of *Original Charleston, Ivy, I Can't Give You Anything But Love,* etc., than as the virtuoso of Brunswick's *Jingles.* Most of these tunes were workaday products tailored to suit the needs of colored revues, for Johnson was still active chiefly in this field. He also did skits and lyrics for production shows at Connie's Inn, for Ziegfeld, Carroll, Schubert, and for the Cotton Club. One of his road shows, *Plantation Days,* did so well in America that it was booked for an extended tour of Europe, and Johnson was several months on the road in England and the Continent.

Back in America once more, Johnson was attracted to Hollywood

by a lucrative offer to do the musical score for the motion picture production *Yamacraw,* starring Bessie Smith.[1] He had already done a great
deal of work with Bessie, as tunesmith and accompanist both on the
road and for record dates.[2] After his scoring had been accepted, he remained in Hollywood long enough to play a supporting part in the
picture.

It is quite impossible to keep up with James P. during the roaring
Twenties. In fact, as he says, he did well to keep up with himself. There
was always something to absorb his interests and manifold talents. A new
show to be rehearsed. Two more sides for Columbia. A short engagement as band pianist. A recording date with Ethel Waters or Roy Evans.
A jam session at the Rhythm Club, where men like Ellington, Hopkins,
Fats and the Lion spoke of "going to get their lessons" from the grandfather. The Louisiana Sugar Babes date for Victor. Giving Fats, James
P.'s boy, a brush-up lesson. Another show in production for the road. To
Hollywood for a Warner Brothers short. Another celluloid role, this
time for Pathe. Sitting in uptown with Bix and Tram and Louis. A
four-week engagement as featured soloist at the Savoy. House rent
parties and chitlin' struts.

Here was a man with vitality and personality, and besides that ability
and perhaps not a little genius. A man who knew everyone, and worked
hard and got his kicks and saved a little money. Looking back, we are
interested mainly in the man's music—his records and the influence
of his piano—but these things were no more than threads in a larger
pattern. We wonder how his records and his piano managed to escape
the taint of commercialism, how he avoided becoming a bizarre medley
of Confrey, Gershwin, and Irving Berlin, how the slender threads in
the disorganized pattern came to acquire lasting form and color after
the rest of the picture had blurred off. Jimmy wonders himself. If he
has succeeded in salvaging something of value from the hectic, too successful career, he believes he owes it to his unflagging interest in after-

---

[1] It is strange that the jazz archeologists who have devoted so much energy to digging up
old records and getting the recording companies to reissue them have never attempted
to get a re-showing, if only at the Museum of Modern Art, of this film, or—at the very
least—had the sound track put on wax where it might give the world a few more Bessie
Smith performances as well as the music and scoring of James P. (ED.)
[2] His best known accompaniment is the beautiful Bessie Smith *Backwater Blues,* Columbia
14195.

hours music. At his busiest, he still found time to play at a house rent party or a jam session. A man with a tremendous vitality can relax at activities which exhaust another. So James P. went uptown to let his hair down and get his kicks; and the field of jazz music is permanently enriched by his efforts.

The fall of Wall Street marked the end of this fabulous decade. Out, with the G notes and the bootleggers and the It girls, went jazz music. Or rather, jazz went underground. And Johnson went home—to the two-storey house he had purchased in the middle-class suburb of Jamaica. He was fortyish, growing a little fat and a little bald. He took up pipe smoking and became quiet and philosophical. He slowed down, yes; but he had no notion he was through. During his career he had been a pianist, entertainer, performer, composer of popular tunes, director of musical comedies, amateur actor, dean of the 88 among the jazz select. But one endeavor had eluded him, piqued his curiosity, challenged his ability. As a busy foreign correspondent might long for leisure in which to write a serious novel, Johnson had dreamed of trying his hand at serious composition.

The *Yamacraw* scoring had sharpened this growing interest and the Thirties finally found Johnson in a position to make a start. Gershwin's attempts to work jazz material into more serious form seemed imperfect to Johnson. Without conceit, he thought himself in a more advantageous position to succeed where Gershwin had failed—or rather, had managed to please only dilettantes. The great library of jazz music, or blues, rags, stomps, fox-trots, popular songs, had a vast wealth of material to offer, Johnson thought. He wanted a form of music which would give more lasting permanence to the material than the transient four-four, 12-and 16-bar structures. So, in the quiet of his home, he sat down at the fine grand piano he had acquired and began his work. He had a big, tough job ahead. He is still at it, and expects to be as long as he lives.

The first serious effort was *Tone Poem*, begun in 1930. In 1932 he completed *Symphony Harlem* (four movements: *Subway Journey, Song of Harlem, Night Club, Baptist Mission*). *St. Louis Blues*, an elaborate improvisation on the Handy classic, followed in 1936. More recently he had been working on the most ambitious job yet, an opus tentatively titled *Symphony in Brown*, which intended to trace out the rise of jazz music. The success of these challenging endeavors remains to be seen. Eugene von Gronna used *Symphony Harlem* for the Negro Ballet, produced at the Lafayette Theatre, New York in 1937. There have been other performances since then. But this music finds itself poised between righteous jazz on the one hand and classical music on the other, subject to all manner of prejudice and suspicion. And it has never been easy for a new composer to interest important men in the classical field with his creations.

If Johnson's story ended here, many hardshelled jazzophiles would be inclined to shake their heads and lament the passing of another one-time great. This judgment might be defensible had James P. remained in complete retirement. Fortunately, his selection as pianist on the important Panassié Bluebird dates of '39 (Mezz Mezzrow Orchestra; Frankie Newton Orchestra) and more specially, his subsequent recording work, have furnished evidence to the contrary. James P. plays a mellower piano these days, but it has lost nothing, in the opinion of this writer. The two opening choruses on his Decca *Stop It, Joe* (Rosetta Crawford) shows that here is still the piano with more *pure swing* than any other in the business, not excepting Hines or Waller—and that with a minimum of effort, with greater economy than ever before. Here is no faded relic or dated exhibit, no tricky musical scholar or effete, meretricious Gershwin. Here literally, freshened by the latest acoustical advances, is the true Grandfather.

After all, a man who remained a top-flight musician while he was being all things to all people in the music business ought to be able to fluff off any softening influences of composing for full symphony. And maybe those more recent and most ambitious efforts will be the bridge, or the foundation for the bridge, between this incredibly rich native music of ours and the more timeless classic forms.

Index

Ablaba, 172
Allen, Henry, Jr., 75, 108
Armstrong, Louis, 2, 4, 9, 20, 61, 68, 72-77, 85, 88, 89, 97-99, 105, 106, 119-22, 128, 141, 143, 152, 155, 165, 166, 168, 174
Avakian, George, 68

Bach, J. S., 2, 13, 15, 26, 39, 59, 67, 117, 138, 143
Bacquet, George (Bakay), 72, 92, 102
Barbarin, Paul, 73, 74, 108
Bartók, Béla, 9
Basie, Count, 4, 159
Bechet, Sidney, 72, 88, 89, 92, 99, 109-11, 118, 120
Beethoven, Ludwig van, 3, 14, 23, 60
Beiderbecke, Bix, 21, 76, 85, 119, 120, 123-36, 141, 152-54, 159, 166-69, 174
Berger, Morroe, 119
Berigan, Bunny, 69
Berlin, Irving, 49, 51, 114n, 174
Bigard, Barney, 5, 72, 74, 75, 109, 144, 145
Black, Lew, 79, 80, 82, 83
Blesh, Rudi, 7
Bocage, Pete, 88, 92, 98
Bolden, Buddy, 87, 88, 96-99, 101, 102, 140
Brahms, Johannes, 3, 113, 152
Braud, Wellman, 75, 109
Briggs, Peter, 75, 76
Brown, Steve, 80-83
Brunis, George, 79-83
Busse, Henry, 2

Carey, Mutt, 71, 88
Carmichael, Hoagy, 85, 123, 124, 127-29
Carter, Benny, 144, 156
Chambers, Tig, 71, 73, 101
Chopin, Frédéric, 5
Colombo, Russ, 70
Condon, Eddie, 4, 85, 93
Conzelman, Bob, 123, 124
Cook, Will Marion, 2, 111, 113, 117
Cooke, Charlie, 74, 75
Crosby, Bing, 70, 121

DeParis, Sidney, 109, 110
Dickerson, Carroll, 74-76, 121
Dodds, Baby, 89, 119, 162

Dodds, Johnny, 61, 72, 74, 107, 108, 119, 120, 166
Dutrey, Honore, 74, 75, 119

Ellington, Duke, 1, 2, 4, 5, 20, 26-29, 75, 84, 95, 102, 105, 120, 137-47, 174
Europe, Lt. Jim, 49, 143, 172
Evans, Stompy, 75, 107

Farley, Mike, 4
Fitzgerald, Ella, 70
Freeman, Bud, 119
Frescobaldi, Girolamo, 1, 12, 13, 111

Gabler, Milt, 4, 6
Gershwin, George, 2, 3, 4, 44, 48, 50, 51, 69, 140, 155, 174-76
Gillespie, Dizzy, 9
Gillette, Bob, 124, 126, 129, 136
Goldkette, Jean, 133, 154, 166
Goodman, Benny, 2, 4, 5, 9, 82-85, 109, 120, 124, 137, 148-61, 163, 165, 166, 168
Greer, Sonny, 144, 145, 147
Grofé, Ferde, 3

Hall, Tubby, 75, 77
Hampton, Lionel, 156, 166
Handel, G. F., 13, 15, 117
Handy, W. C., 30-55, 93, 100, 140
Hardin, Lil (Mrs. L. Armstrong), 73, 74, 119
Harney, Ben, 50, 172
Hartwell, Jimmy, 124, 135
Haydn, Josef, 13, 14, 15, 22, 122
Held, John, 2
Henderson, Fletcher, 74, 76, 77, 84, 95, 120, 121, 143, 148, 158
Hines, Earl, 73, 75, 121, 122, 143, 168, 176
Hodges, Johnny, 69
Holiday, Billie, 69-71, 121
Hunter, Albert, 44n, 54

Jackson, Preston, 71-77, 99n
Jackson, Tony, 101, 103
James, Harry, 4
Johnson, Bill, 72, 74, 102, 108
Johnson, Bunk, 4, 6, 5, 68, 88, 89, 91, 95-99, 137
Johnson, George, 123, 136

Johnson, James P., 68, 165, 168, 170-76
Johnson, James Weldon, 45n, 55, 94
Johnson, Pete, 58, 60

Keppard, Freddie, 71-75, 78, 87, 101, 102
Khatchaturian, Aram, 3
Kirby, John, 6
Kostelanetz, André, 5
Krupa, Gene, 85, 149, 150, 158, 163, 165, 168

Ladnier, Tommy, 73, 76, 106
LaRocca, Nick, 72, 99, 141
Leibrook, Min, 125, 126, 135
Lewis, Meade ("Lux"), 56-60
Lindsay, John, 77, 105, 106
Lopez, Vincent, 4
Lunceford, Jimmy, 5

Marable, Fate, 87, 165
Mares, Paul, 73, 78-83, 133, 168
Maugars, André, 12, 13
Mezzrow, Mezz, 7, 122, 153, 176
Miley, Bubber, 24-29
Milhaud, Darius, 3, 14, 65
Miller, Ray, 131, 132
Mitchell, George, 105-8
Moore, Vic, 123, 126, 128-30, 135, 136
Morton, Ferdinand ("Jelly Roll"), 1, 73, 78, 87,
    92n, 95, 100-103, 104-10, 120, 170
Mozart, W. A., 13, 14, 118, 152, 160, 161
Mulligan, Gerry, 8
Murray, Don, 81, 124

Nanton, Tricky Sam, 20, 26, 27
Nelson, "Big Eye" Louis, 88, 90, 92, 96-99
Nicholas, Albert, 72, 74, 75, 108-10
Nichols, Red, 131-33, 141, 154
Noone, Jimmy, 73-75, 105, 120

Oliver, King, 2, 71-77, 78, 85, 87, 85, 97, 99,
    102, 105, 119-20, 128, 152
Ory, Kid, 61, 72, 74, 75, 88, 95, 105, 106

Palmer, Bea, 79, 134
Perez, Manuel, 71, 92, 97-99
Picou, Alphonse, 88, 90, 92, 96-98, 110
Pollack, Ben, 80, 82, 83, 121, 142, 153, 155
Porter, Cole, 70

Pound, Ezra, 10
Previn, André, 8

Qualey, Dan, 56, 63

Rainey, Ma, 52, 54, 68
Rapollo, Leon, 73, 78-83, 154
Roberts, Lucky, 168, 171, 172
Robinson, Fred, 76, 109
Robinson, Jim, 89, 90
Riley, Ed, 4
Russell, Luis, 73, 75, 108
Russell, William, 4

St. Cyr, Johnny, 105-7, 119
Sandburg, Carl, 3
Sartre, Jean-Paul, 64
Schoebel, Elmer, 73, 78-81, 83
Shaw, Artie, 6, 69
Shostakovich, Dimitri, 3
Simeon, Omer, 75, 104-8
Singleton, Zutty, 75, 76, 109, 110
Smith, Bessie, 28, 54, 69-71, 163, 174
Smith, Joe, 68, 120
Smith, Mamie, 10
Smith, Pine Top, 61, 165, 168
Spanier, Muggsie, 71, 85
Stacey, Jess, 5
Stiedry, Fritz, 6
Stokowski, Leopold, 3, 158, 159
Stravinsky, Igor, 3, 9, 60, 112

Tate, Erskine, 74, 75
Teagarden, Jack, 76, 142
Teschmaker, Frank, 78, 108, 153
Toledano, Ralph de, 1
Trumbauer, Frankie, 131, 133, 141, 174

Voynow, Dick, 123-25, 136

Walker, Frank, 68
Waller, Fats, 121, 174, 176
Watters, Lu, 89, 95
Whiteman, Paul, 2, 3, 4, 30, 47, 102, 139, 141,
    142, 155
Williams, Cootie, 5
Williams, Eugene, 4, 88, 89, 106n, 162
Wilson, Teddy, 69, 156, 166, 167